I0086347

The Guyland

#

JERRY SANDER

© 2022 The Way It Works Press

The Guyland is where I began to grow up.

Names have been changed to protect the innocent and the partially innocent.

Some memories have been enhanced and altered for the sake of larger emotional truths.

"The music is not in the notes, but in the silence between."

– WOLFGANG AMADEUS MOZART

To
Lillian Ketcham

Contents

#

My First Job

# #

I woke up and – for the first time ever – my mother was gone. My father was making pancakes.

"You have a baby sister," he said, serving me breakfast with butter slathered over the lightly-browned circles. He poured Log Cabin syrup over the top. I'd never seen my father cook before. Later, I would watch as he made fried-banana and peanut-butter sandwiches for himself, something none of us ever wanted to try. Too weird.

"Where's Mom?" I asked.

"She's in the hospital. I'm going over to get her and the baby soon. You'll stay here with Daisy. We'll all be together later."

I went out to play and told George Benton I was getting a sister. I hadn't known you had to go to a hospital to get a baby sister.

"Do you know that if you eat snow, it could kill you, because the Russians put poison in the clouds?" George asked.

I didn't know what he was talking about.

"What about babies?" I asked.

"It would kill them, too."

"No, I mean… do you have a baby in your house? Brother or a sister?" I asked.

"Yeah, a brother."

"Is he fun?"

"He cries a lot. He poops all the time. But … he's little. I think they get better," he said. "You have to protect them.

That's your job. You're the big brother. Like if anyone picks on them, you smash the guy in the face."

I knew this already. I don't know how I knew, or who told me, but it wasn't George.

"I'm going to protect my sister her whole life," I said.

I didn't wonder what my father's job was if mine was to protect my sister. I knew my father's job. He was a pharmacist. He put medicine in bottles for people and then put labels on so that they would get better. It took a lot of hours away at the store; I could cover for him at home.

The Devil

# #

They said you could wear your costume to school on Halloween of first grade. Halloween was on a Thursday, and we were going to have a party starting at 10:45 a.m. Then there was a costume parade around Sherwood Elementary at noon. Parents were invited to come, and my mother was coming. My father had to work. You could bring in cookies, donuts, cakes, and little packages of Hi-C or Hawaiian Punch, as long as you brought in enough to share with everyone, and you could also bring in Dixie cups and most of all, napkins.

I wanted to be Fred Flintsone for Halloween, but when we went to the costume store my mother took me to didn't have any left. I asked about The Rifleman and the saleslady said they didn't have any of him, either.

That's when I saw and fell in love with the full-length devil suit. It was standing directly across from us on a store statue about my size. It came with a large, red, three-pronged pitchfork, a little black cape with red on the inside, horns, and a scary plastic beard mask. I didn't have to try it on. I knew I wanted it, right away. My mother read the back of the box; it was my size. It would fit.

Thursday came and my mother made brownies for the class, along with an orange-flavored punch that had black-licorice straws sticking out of it so the whole punchbowl looked like a witch's brew.

I came downstairs for breakfast before school in the costume and presented myself to my father and sister, who hadn't seen it yet.

"Da-DA!" I announced, turning slowly, messing with the cape, swooping it around in a slow circle and looking scary.

"Who are you supposed to be?" my sister asked.

My father said, "Stand still while I get the camera."

My mother came up behind me, circling me with her arms and joining her hands at my belly. She pulled me closer and leaned in, hugging me close, her face next to mine as I held my pitchfork out, menacing all who crossed my path. My breath in the mask was warm. I could hear my tail flopping behind me when I walked. My mask-beard gave me a perfect dark *T*. I felt and loved my devil-powers.

The flashbulb went off and the picture was taken. My father chuckled softly.

We saw the picture a week later. In it, my mother's eyes were gleaming red. She must have been feeling the devil powers too, streaming up through my feet, all the way to the outer reaches of my fingers and pitchfork. Her arms were wrapped around me and her smile matched her eyes. She was thrilled, as if the powers belonged to her.

Frankie Valli

#

It was the summer after I'd turned ten. Fourth grade.

The sun was strong. Seagulls swooped low, then high. Beach umbrellas opened all around us, a strong *Pop,!* followed by the sound of fabric giving quiet shade.

We had just our blanket and towels. We faced the sun together. It baked us from on high. It had to be close to noon.

I stripped off my shirt. I peeled off my jeans. I had my Hawaiian-print longboard turquoise bathing suit on underneath. I wished I wasn't chubby. Other kids weren't.

My mother popped open the large brown plastic Coppertone, squirted some into one hand, rubbed her hands together and then reached over for the top of my right shoulder. Her left hand went to my left shoulder. She rubbed vigorously. "Hold still," she said. I could feel my skin getting the cooling lotion, and I imagined it sinking in. My shoulders relaxed.

In the distance, a small radio played Frankie Valli and the Four Seasons. It was "Rag Doll." It felt like, I guessed, the 1950s did, down at the beach. The waves pounded, and there were squeals from some little kids at the surf's edge.

"You burn easily. All it takes is one burn…"

She applied the sharp and cool smelling lotion to my face, holding my cheeks with both hands for a second, then smearing it in. I felt like laughing. I wanted this to last forever.

"You do the rest. Remember: every ninety minutes. More often if you go in. The sun is unforgiving," she said.

"Especially if you are uncovered."

I nodded.

"Don't forget your toes," she said.

In the ice cooler next to her was a peanut butter and jelly sandwich (Skippy, the crunchy kind, with Welch's grape jelly), a container of Hawaiian Punch, a plum, and two Chips Ahoy cookies. She'd brought some kind of health-food bar that looked terrible for herself.

I sat down next to her. The birds swooped over the waves and because of the wind, we felt the sea spray after each wave crashed. Smaller birds went running along the line where the waves fell back, and we watched them poke at things in the sand, quickly swallowing whatever it was they had found.

The sun wasn't unforgiving. Not today, with the lotion on and my mother at my side. Together, with the wind and the water, it was just right.

Better than a movie.

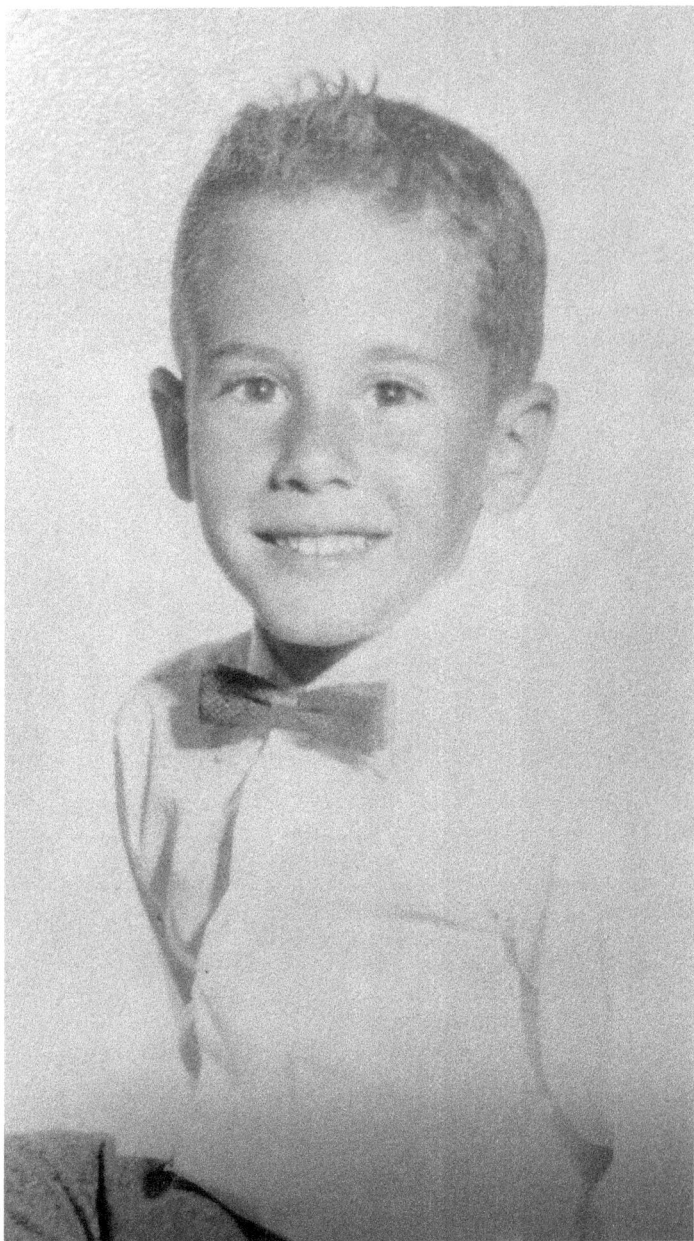

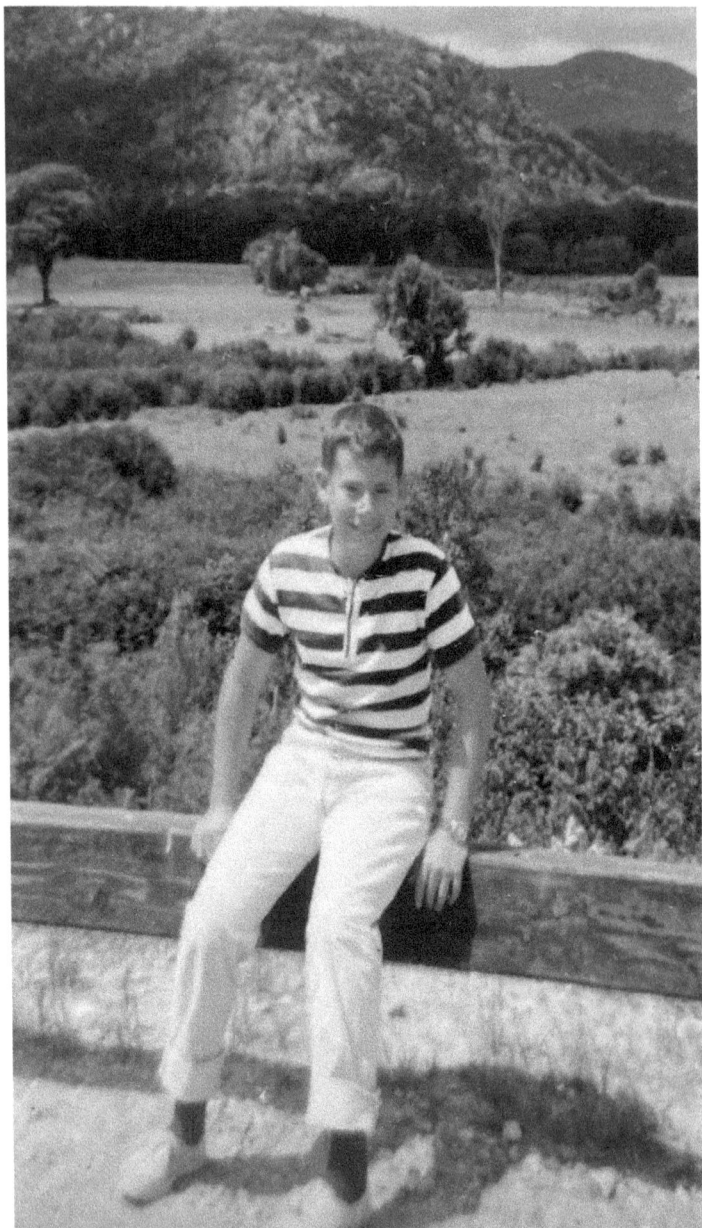

Ladies & Gentlemen, The Beatles (Part 1)

# #

Seventh grade started next week, but next week was next week, which was the next best thing to never.

No one had a girlfriend. You didn't need one.

Gary and I were going to camp out on his back lawn in the pup tent. It was his brother's, but he didn't use it anymore. Gary aired it out two days in advance. I stole my father's July issue of *Playboy* and Gary stole two warm cans of Pabst Blue Ribbon from somewhere. He also had a huge flashlight, M-80's, two cherry bombs, and six bottle rockets leftover from the Fourth of July,, so we were all set. We would stay up all night and roam the town, if we felt like it. Neither of us was afraid of the dark.

Alyssa Pantucci – who had a bad track record for coming anywhere near the truth whenever she opened her mouth – had spread the rumor that when NASA did the second Gemini spacewalk, the astronauts saw a monster ghost and might have brought it back with them when they returned. The government knew about it and was trying to figure out how to break it to us, she told us.

Alone in the tent, Gary and I talked about the crisis with The Beatles. We had been third graders when we first saw them on *Ed Sullivan* shaking their long hair around, closing in while the music was pumping to sing into the same shared microphone. That was a long, long time ago. Kids weren't sure The Beatles would last until seventh grade. There was some new, good evidence that kids might be right.

"John said they were more popular than Jesus two weeks ago," I said. "Doris Schofmeister said he's going to go to hell. Or he'll die under unusual circumstances. Ricky Shmick said The Beatles will definitely break up this year. But I think it's just going to make them even bigger."

Gary listened. "Jesus didn't have girls mailing him their panties. The Beatles do. Who would *you* rather be?"

"They get mailed panties?" I asked. "Who said that? I never read that."

"Frank Leschick."

"How does *he* know?" I asked.

"His cousin works in the city in the same building as their record company," Gary answered.

"But that doesn't mean he sees their mail, right?" I pointed out.

"Why would he make that up, though? To his own cousin?" Gary rebutted. "Think about it."

I did. I thought about the girls in my class – blonde-haired Christine Mendishak, Leola Montlani, and the very well-organized and well-behaved, dark-haired Penelope Firestone. Each one of them wore panties; maybe not even the same color. It was hard to imagine them sending them away to The Beatles.

Gary and I contemplated Frank Leschick's cousin's information silently.

"You saw Christine's that one time, right?" he asked. "What color were they?"

I knew what he was talking about. How could I forget? It was when Christine was leaning over next to my desk on the right side and I was putting my books on the rack under my seat while looking left, and talking to the kid next to me. I brought my hand up first and it lifted up her skirt by accident all the way to her waist for two crazy seconds. Someone saved me from getting punched in the nose or beaten to a pulp as I was saying I was innocent.

A sixth grade riot almost broke out. It really was an accident, but it was a memorable one.

"Pink," I said.

"Oh, man…oh *man* … they *would* be pink, right? That just *goes* with her, right?" Gary looked excited, like he had more to express, but couldn't figure out how.

"What color do you think Penelope's are?" I asked.

Gary pondered this. "Blue?" he asked, as if I knew the answer.

"I'm thinking turquoise," I ventured. "That would be *so hot…*"

Suddenly the thought occurred to me, about the girls in my class: Maybe they already *had* mailed their panties away, and were just *looking* normal in class. It's not like they were ever going to admit it, and it's not like I was going to ask. I wondered if their moms had noticed when she did their laundry that one pair of panties was missing. Girls could be so sneaky.

"The Beatles are okay, but Kevin says there's a new band that's better," Gary said.

"The Rolling Stones?" I asked.

"No. They're called The Doors."

I laughed. "That's a stupid name. Never heard of them."

"They have an album. Kevin has it. It just came out," Gary explained.

Gary, Kevin, and I – when we were back in third grade – had mixed feelings about The Beatles anyway. The fact that the girls all thought they were cute and knew all their names meant we had to automatically oppose them and declare them stupid. Songs like "Yellow Submarine" were just latter-day proof of our rightness. The Beatles were for babies. And no one I knew wanted to live in a yellow submarine.

"How come Kevin has all this money to buy albums?" I asked.

"Both his parents work," Gary offered.

"That's kind of weird," I said. "His mother, too? So they're rich?"

"He has to make dinner for himself sometimes," Gary said, "But he can eat whatever he feels like." We pondered this. We had gone over to Kevin's' house to watch *Star Trek* in color; they were the first ones to have a color TV in our town. It was totally different, seeing things in color. It was like being there. Kevin's house also had a finished basement, so after we watched TV upstairs, we brought snacks downstairs and played Risk. I always started by building up armies in Africa and South America, saving Europe for my final conquest.

It had slowly gotten dark while we were talking and we hunkered down in the tent, turning on the flashlight and shining it on the back wall of the tent so it wasn't in our faces. Crickets were loud. It was nice to have nothing to do. The *Playboy* magazine was very much on my mind, but I wanted to savor it and take it out only at the right time. This was talking time.

"Do you know Brianna Gader on Bay 3rd Street?" I asked.

"No. Wait – maybe. Does she have a sister, Gabby?"

"Gabby Gader? Yeah, that's her," I said.

"Gabby threw up on our lawn last year. They were driving somewhere, I guess, and the car pulled over, she opened the door and hurled. I don't know why they couldn't have made it home for her to puke. It's two blocks away," he said. "And the worst thing?" he asked.

"Yeah?" I said.

"It was blue and orange."

"Probably Italian ices? Or a 7-11 slushie?" I guessed.

"I don't know, but it was gross," Gary said. "I brought out cat litter from the garage and threw it over it."

"Good thinking," I said. "Anyway, Gabby's sister, Brianna? She used to be ugly, now I don't think she is."

"How come?" he asked.

"When she wore these white shorts. Maybe she grew too fast, or something, but she's really tall now and she was wearing these white shorts and I looked and ... she was *all legs*. Really smooth-looking legs. They just keep going and going. Her face is getting better, too."

"Like she's growing into it or something?" Gary asked.

"Yeah. I don't know, can you grow into your face?"

"Yes, you can," Gary clarified. "You can definitely grow into a face."

"So we're probably growing into ours?" I asked.

"No, I think we already have them," he said.

"Girls grow into their breasts, too, right?" I asked.

"Well, that's more breasts growing into the girl," he said.

"'Onto' them, not 'into' them. Or 'out of them.' 'Into them' would be gross ... it's like dicks," I offered.

"What's like dicks?"

"Them growing."

He contemplated this. "No. It's not like dicks. We already have dicks. Breasts are a whole different thing."

"But they're all still growing, right?" I clarified.

"Yeah, everything grows," Gary said. "At some point, it all stays the same. But not yet."

And everything dies, I thought. *Just like my grandpa did last year*. But I didn't say it.

"The thing about Brianna – getting back to her – is that she still acts like she used to. Before her breasts. Mysterious."

"Girls are uncomfortable at this age. You have to leave them alone. They stay mysterious until the mood passes," Gary explained.

When he talked this way, I knew, it was because of his sister, Janine, who went to SUNY Stony Brook. He just wasn't capable of sentences like that. "Sometimes it takes years," he went on. "Some girls it's forever. Just leave those ones alone. Oh my God. Speaking of mysterious – actually *weird*: As in 'No way! Weird': You heard about Sunny Tolson?" Gary offered, eyes sparkling.

That's when we heard a big *bang* sound from the inside of his house. "What was that?" I asked.

Gary looked like he was familiar with the sound. "My mother."

I waited for more.

"She throws things. Only when she's mad."

"What makes her mad?" I asked.

"My father," he offered.

"What does she throw?"

"Usually his stuff," he said. "She doesn't ... y'know, it's just ... that's the way they are."

I knew that his parents, Barry and Sherry Dart, played tennis doubles down at the BayWay Beach Club and were famous for their meltdowns, thrown racquets, and public scenes. I'd seen it once myself, and it was thrilling in an embarrassing way, as I hadn't seen adults behave this way. "When you play net, Sherry, you *play the net*. Anything overhead, you don't drop back. I've got it. I'm playing *the rest*."

"You're playing *nothing*!" she screamed. "It's all up to me, all the time, Barry! Are you even paying attention? No! What were you doing? Looking at the teen girls walking to the pool? Tracking some cute butts?"

It's true; that's exactly what he'd been doing. Me, too.

"Do you wanna go on over there and introduce yourself to them? Hire some babysitters?" she yelled.

"Give it up, Sherry! Is that you or the booze talking?" Barry shot back.

"Takes one to know one," she screamed, before the wife of the other couple they were playing against walked over to her, approached her at the net, and put her arm around Sherry. The woman whispered something quietly to her.

I watched Barry's face get red, and then he walked two steps to the right before turning around, muttering, walking to the back, turning around, bouncing the ball four of five times, and muttering some more.

The girls on the way to the pool were impressive. They were about three or four years older than me, and they were on the swim team. They seemed to know that everyone was looking at them and that they were some sort of *pack* of well-exercised, long-haired beauties in red one-piece Speedos. I left Sherry and Barry and found some excuse to walk by the pool casually, seeing them stretch, put their hair up in buns before pulling on their swim caps and then ever so purposefully,snap the lower band of the bottom their suits into place, snapping and releasing, which allowed for the most perfectly view of strong teenage female bodies I'd ever seen in my life. I think I stopped breathing before I realized I'd better keep moving or else it would look like I was looking at them.

In the tent that night, I thought back to all of this and it seemed extremely alive to me. I asked Gary, in my most casual voice, "Do you have that *Playboy* magazine?"

"After beer," Gary said, pulling out the warm cans of Pabst. We both tried to look like this was no big deal, just something *we do* now and then, popping the tab, but it was my first time and – for all I know – his, too. I moved to pop open the top and it took a bunch of effort. I was afraid it made me look lame – I wasn't used to these pop-tabs; my main drink was Hawaiaan Punch from a pitcher my mom kept on the top shelf – but I felt better to see that Gary was struggling with his can's top, too. Finally they went and the tent got spritzed with warm jets of cheap, stolen Pabst Blue Ribbon beer. We settled down and sipped our cans.

I immediately wanted to gag; it tasted and smelled like something in between what I imagined a bucket of rusty rainwater with a nail at the bottom of it might taste like and a warm soda made with puke. I couldn't believe this was it: The Big Kahuna, what adults craved and loved while we weren't allowed to drink it. *Bleccchhhhh…*

"What were you going to say about Sunny Tolson?" I asked. "Before your mother threw something…"

He took a big slug. "You're not going to believe me," he said confidently.

"Try me," I shot back.

"It's a waste of time, I *know* you're not going to believe this."

"Is it the truth?"

"Well, yeah," Gary said confidently.

"Then why wouldn't I believe you?"

"Because it's so… out of the ordinary," he said. "It's like magic. You know the possibility of it exists, but it's probably not really there, just a man doing tricks he learned from a kit or a book for a children's party. But what if it were real? And it happened? And no one even saw it for real?"

I thought about this. This was a good point. We were so used to fake things that we wouldn't know it if something real came along.

"You know Sunny Tolson, right?" he asked, after another big gulp of beer. I tried to follow him by taking a gulp myself.

"Yes, I already said yes. She plays flute, in eighth grade band," I said, conjuring up the image of her delicate face, bright blue eyes peering over glasses to follow Mr. Melangrino as he conducted the pretty terrible sounding concert band, trying to push them through Leroy Anderson's "Sleigh Ride." Sunny was one of the big kids, about to go into ninth grade.

"Okay," Gary said, his voice getting lower as he inched closer, moving his sleeping bag with him. "Anne Littit, another eighth grader, had this party about a week ago. Obviously, you and I weren't invited, and there weren't *any* fifth graders there. At that party…" he said, pausing to refuel with a long glug of Pabst. "At that party, which went on *all night* and at which, I am told her parents were *nowhere in sight* because they were in the Finger Lakes, she went upstairs."

"Sunny?" I asked.

"Yes, Sunny," he said definitively. "She goes upstairs, it turns midnight, and at the stroke of midnight, with everyone looking, she comes downstairs slowly, walking down the staircase *totally nude*."

"No," I concluded.

"No meaning '*yes*,'" he said, forcibly. "This *happened*."

"Yeah?" I asked. "There were multiple witnesses?"

"Multiple," he said.

"*Totally* nude," I said.

"Yes. Well – actually – she was wearing white athletic socks and sneakers. So I don't know if that counts. But – otherwise – *yes*," Gary swore.

It took a minute for this image to sink in. Sink in, it did.

"Why would she do that? Whether she did or didn't," I asked. "It doesn't make any sense."

"I know. I told you: It's like magic. Magic is better than sense," Gary said, looking wise for the briefest moment.

"Maybe not magic, maybe like lightning," I offered.

"Lightning just striking."

The truth is that neither of us really knew what a nude woman looked like. Gary said that he saw his mother changing once, but that she had her underwear on the whole time, anyway. We knew girls' bodies were different than ours, but we just drew a blank, basically, trying to get some mileage out of presuming we *knew*. We knew they had butts, and I had deducted that the rest was pretty different than us. But I had no idea about the details.

"Let's see the magazine," I ventured, still marinating in the lingering images of Sunny in her athletic socks slowly descending the staircase enough to feel the stirrings of my boner.

"Sure," Gary said, "Did you know they *always have* to have a rabbit on the cover? But it's sometime disguised? Like ... look at this!" he said, laying the cover in front of me. The lower half of a deliciously tanned woman in a black bikini, laying on a white beach towel was in front of me, next to the words "A Toast to Bikinis." No, I couldn't see a rabbit, and I didn't need to.

"It's where they tied her bikini, on the side," he said, pointing to some little rabbit-like ears. I was deep into study, trying to figure out what was beneath the black fabric. I never was good at noticing little details.

Gary flipped past all the letters to the editor, the articles, the pictures of this month's contributors – men with pipes in their mouths, beards, berets, turtlenecks, and blazers – until the bursting colors of the women inside commanded us. The colors and textures of their bodies were radiant. They lifted themselves off the page in the direction of our flashlight while somehow at the same time, inviting us to merge downward with them, leaving the world of this beer-smelling pup-tent and parents with rules and things that they threw to join them in some naughty fun. These women's bodies were *just waiting* for seventh graders to attend to them.

"Oh my God," Gary said, turning the page to reveal a completely topless shot of Pam, a co-ed at the University of Alabama, her see-through fake-pajama top (tied at the top, but open to show her breasts, and hands demurely placed so that we couldn't see whatever existed between her legs while she smiled with pearly white teeth and a clear invitation to join her. "Oh my God," Gary repeated, turning to look at me directly. "Doesn't it make you *wanna*?"

Yes, it did. But we didn't know *wanna what*. He wasn't talking about humping your pillow, and he wasn't talking about playing pocket pool. He was talking about *doing it,,* whatever *it* was to be done. He was talking about whether it made you *wanna* or not, and the answer was yes.

I was trying to merge this with my fascination for the girls in our class and their panties. What exactly did I think would happen, anyway? If anything were to happen? If Nicky liked me?

We flipped through some more pictures. They all had women with their big, beautiful, juicy breasts displayed, while the women were smiling devilishly. None of the pictures had that middle area below the belly displayed. That's when I put it together for the first time: human reproduction – pregnancy – had something to do with our dicks and women's breasts. That's how it all happens, I'd bet. I looked over and Gary and pondered telling him my realization.

"Want to blow off some bottle rockets?" Gary asked with a glint in his eye.

PF Flyers

# #

Keds looked good, but PF Flyers not only looked cooler, they let you run faster and jump higher. They were the ones that went up over your ankle and were blue. Under the blue was a thin red stripe all around it, and under that was the white that covered the springy parts. So they technically were red, white, and blue, and I couldn't help but think that they had some special American powers that went with them because of this. All this *plus* the faster and higher power made these, the PF Flyers, the only choice for spring of eighth grade.

The weekend after the new sneakers went on sale, my mother took me to Gimbel's and we bought a pair. The man said I was up almost an entire size and a half from my old Keds. I stepped on the weird, flounder-shaped thing and he said, "Put your weight on it; you're not putting your weight on it." I was either too considerate of the device or wanted to feel less fat. I tried making the adjustment on the measuring device and he said, "Just stand naturally on your foot. Don't force it." I couldn't figure out what he meant by "stand naturally."

Eventually we figured it out enough to be able to buy them, and he asked if I wanted to wear them out of the store. I said yes. We threw my old Keds away. I looked at them going into the garbage can at the store, and I thought of all the times I played baseball in them and rode my bicycle all over town in them last year. It felt scary to part with them.

The first thing I did when I got home was try the fence

at the end of Sherwood Drive. It was true; the jump to a high point of the wire fence, and the subsequent haul over it – complete with newly-padded landing, was stronger and required much less effort. It might not be exactly the same as having super powers, but it was a major step toward them.

The girls of Bay 3rd Street were basically sisters of kids we knew, or new kids who had moved in and who kept to themselves. That meant no one was exactly bursting with personality. Nothing stood out about them. You could easily imagine them on long car rides with you, crossing over to your side of the back seat just moments after you drew the line and made it clear whose side was whose. They were as curvaceous as ironing boards, which promoted much puzzlement as we'd all seen our fathers' *Playboys*, which didn't feature girls / women who looked like snarly ironing boards. Maybe she'd lifted her skirt up on purpose with someone, somewhere, we thought, and she was still getting over it. Maybe she was going to blush because she thought we knew all about it.

It was a Thursday, and my parents had a Thursday through Sunday membership at BayWay Beach Club. The place was paradise for any eighth-grade boy who wanted documentary proof that girls in bikinis existed, beyond the pages of *Playboy*. These girls were usually older than us, of course, but that was okay.

BayWay Beach Club always smelled of greasy burgers, hot dogs, and fries. You had to wait in line in the sun until you approached the counter and could order. They also had irresistible add-ons that included frozen Milky Way bars, Fudgsicles, popcorn, and pretzels. The jukebox in the room across the path played "96 Tears," "A Little Bit O' Soul," "Day Tripper," and "Good Lovin'." Standing in line waiting for the sixteen year-olds working behind the counter to get the orders right meant you could be hanging out – in the sun –

with a girl in a two-piece or even bikini while listening to cool music and getting your food in a minute. Half my suntan that summer came from waiting on that line. It was a Saturday, there was no homework to be done, and it was seventy-seven degrees out at noon.

An older girl stood in front of me, the smell of Coppertone on her bronzing skin, combined with the smell of grease and the sound of the Farfisa organ blaring as the guy sang something about teardrops and hearts crying. It was the strongest shot of bliss I'd known in my fourteen and a half years. It was proof of God.

Being awkward yet inventive I had found a way to run around with a 35 mm. camera – a Beseler-Topcon Super-D – and officially have permission to gawk at my peers while employed without pay for the Buccaneer middle school yearbook. This allowed me to attend all dances in order to document them for our future while not having to ask girls to dance and get turned down.

The girls were gathered in small groups anyway, so asking one of them to dance meant leaving your own small group of guys, walking across a dead zone of space with the girls looking, then asking a girl in front of the entire group of them before getting turned down, and walking back, trying to look as if it all didn't matter and was just an ironic joke to have asked anyway.

At the Spring Fling, while supposedly snapping pictures of the decorations, I noticed that Caitlin Murphy seemed to be growing like a weed. Why did these girls always grow faster than us? Her sudden tallness once again seemed to be something she was ready to blush about, as if it were the sexiest thing in the world. I had no idea what went on in her mind all day. I truly couldn't imagine what went on in *most* girls' minds, but hers most of all.

If you asked her if she was taking French or Spanish next year (and I did) she'd answer, "Spanish," and then blush. I'd never imagined that discussion of course selection for next year would give me an erection, but there it was. The fact that I knew nothing about her beyond her grade and what part of town she lived in, made it more powerful. It was amped up, somehow, by the curl in her lip and the mischievous flash in her eyes that she sometimes revealed. I think she was an average student. Since I hung out with the brainiacs – whether I belonged there or not – meant that she was exotic to me. Or dangerous. Or both.

I have five pictures of Caitlin from the Spring Fling. Two were accidental captures that were supposed to be centered on the decorations, but that she was near. She was in the lower right corner of those two, only partially turned towards the camera. One was blurry, and one was of the back of her as she was walking to get punch. The final one, though, was a masterpiece. Her about to blush was caught forever in time, in 1/125 of a second, f2.8, front-on, head turned up and slightly away, as if her own beauty (which was increasing by the moment) was something she hadn't figured out how to handle, or was just going to cause trouble.

Which it did.

Not that she did.

But it did. We did.

Not many kids wanted to hang out for too long in front of the cabana areas – really just a few square feet of sand – with their parents, bright red ice cooler chests, lounge chairs, and too-large sunglasses. We wanted to find each other, not hang out with our families, so we wandered. We discovered all the nooks and crannies of the place – the path in between the back of the guest lounge building and the snack bar, and the narrow space in between the fence and the storage sheds.

It was the summer of my long turquoise Hawaiian bathing suit. It had a Velcro fly in addition to some string that tied at the top of it, which kind of made me nervous because Velcro hadn't been a proven thing as far as I was concerned in bathing suits. It required extra checking. None of us had forgotten what happened to Steve Roche (who would become the first drummer in my first band) at Anne Littit's birthday pool party last month when he looked down and saw his Velcro fly wide open, flapping in the wind. So the jury was still out on Velcro and whether it was a friend of eighth grade boys or not.

This particular late Thursday morning, Connor DeMarco swung by the front of our purple and green cabana to collect me before we walked three doors down and got Gary. Gary was out in front of his parent's cabana with a white unplugged Fender electric guitar trying to learn "Last Train to Clarksville." Since it was unplugged, we couldn't really tell if he'd learned it or not, but he seemed happy. He was acting like he'd mastered it, anyway.

"You're not gonna believe this," Connor said, excited. "You've gotta swear secrecy, okay? You're the only ones I trust with this."

"What?" Gary and I asked at the same time.

"Come with me," Connor said, leading the way with determination.

Gary put the guitar away and we peeled off on the unknown mission.

There was another narrow space – in between the back of the general locker rooms and the tall chain link fence – and it wasn't wide enough to accommodate the average adult. But we weren't average adults by any measure and we squeezed in easily.

"Check this out," Connor said, pointing with his left

hand, grandly, delivering us the present. It was a hole in the wall, just about chest-level. "Tell me what you see."

Gary did the honors. He bent over, pressing his nose against the wood. It wasn't five seconds before he whispered, very quietly, "OhmyGod. No way."

"Way," Connor said.

"What is it?" I asked.

"The girls' locker room," he whispered authoritatively.

I froze. "Who's in there?" I asked as softly as I could muster.

He looked again. "Marie Shuback," he said, mouthing the words quietly.

This couldn't be happening. Marie Shuback was not just cute, she was off-the-charts cute. She and I had been through many hot physical encounters, in all states of nakedness, in my own mind, and in my own bed, late on school nights and weekends when my parents were out of earshot. Sometimes it was in her bed. Or on the beach, not far from where I was now standing. In my mind, yes, but *strongly in my mind. Persistently in my mind.*

Marie was the one who made a habit of accidentally dropping her weekly Top 5 Cute Boys list on the ground in class way back in sixth grade, leaving us to scramble to recover her list of secrets before she could. I frequently made an appearance on that list, but you never knew if your rank went up or down, thus the urgency to get it before she could grab it back. It didn't occur to me until years later that she wasn't trying that hard to recover it.

"Is she getting changed?" I asked.

"Hold on. Too early to tell," Gary said. "Could go either way."

We waited, tense.

"I don't think so. She's messing around with her hair,"

he whispered. "Your turn," he said, suddenly turning to me, gesturing.

I balked. I wanted to – a lot – but I froze. "I thought we were going to play Smash," I said to them both. Smash was a game played on the outdoor handball court; we used tennis racquets and smashed the ball as hard as we could, hoping it'd ricochet off the wall and hit the other guy before he could defend himself.

"Are you kidding?" Connor asked. "We can play Smash anytime. Right here some of your favorite girls you know are getting naked and putting on bathing suits about five feet in front of you. You don't want to look?"

I thought it was sneaky. And if they really *did* get naked, and you got a boner, then what? This didn't seem like the right place. My room alone at night was sexier. This felt like stealing.

"Well, I'm getting another look," Connor said, smashing his nose up against it and peering through.

After he was quiet for a while, Gary asked, "What do you see?"

"Oh man... you'll just have to wonder," Connor said before he finally pulled away from it. "C'mon, let's go to the handball court," he said sharply. For a second he sounded like a dad on a summer trip somewhere. We walked away quickly from the secret spot, trying to look as innocent as we could.

"I have to get my camera," I lied, wanting some time away from both of them. "I told them at school I'd have summer pictures for the yearbook." That was pretty much true. What was also true was that I needed time to myself to figure out if we'd done anything wrong.

"What, do you get *extra credit* for that in some class?" Connor shot back. "Why are you such a good boy all the time?"

27

Gary blurted out, "He's not like that all the time."

"You do like girls, right?" Connor asked. "Not boys?"

"I like your mother," I said, "and I would've had her last night, but the dogs beat me to her."

"Whoa, such gaylord humor! Please stop!" Connor said, moving away from me fast, which is what I wanted.

"No problem," I said, walking away gladly.

I took the long way home to the cabana. My mother and sister were there. My mother was slathering my sister up in Sea & Ski 40 SPF. She looked like a large chicken about to go into the oven.

"Having fun yet?" I asked her.

"Shut up," she said quickly.

My mother looked up. "You're going to get burned. Let me put some cream on you right now."

"No thanks," I said, grabbing my camera from the shelf and a windbreaker from the back of our changing area.

"All it takes is one bad burn and you are predisposed for life," my mother, a school psychologist, said. She always chose the biggest word she could find. It was something they must have taught her in school psychologist classes.

" 'Predisposed' for what?" I asked.

"Cancer," she said, smoothing even more glop onto the remaining visible parts of my sister's body.

"I'm going to live dangerously," I said, walking away fast.

"You're going to regret it," my mother said, clearly annoyed.

"What's for dinner?" I asked, knowing that that was the one thing I could say that would annoy her even more.

Wearing the Beseler Topcon Super D around my neck made me feel more secure and official in one way or another. The camera was built like a tank and had, in fact, been used by the U.S. Navy for combat missions. Was I on a combat mission? There *was* a job I was supposed to do: take pictures of people doing things that looked happy and natural for the yearbook. And of scenery looking scenic.

I wore my windbreaker because it complimented my Hawaiian bathing suit – at least in my mind – and hid a little bit of chub that I was self-conscious about if I were to run into girls.

I rounded the path toward the pool, looking for pictures to take and came up empty. I had taken them all before. The bay, the sand, the summer hats, the seagulls.

Then on the wooden deck jutting out into the bay, I saw Theresa Riley – one of my fellow yearbook staff kids from school – laying in the sun wearing a pink two-piece. I had no previous pictures of her, so I headed her way.

I stopped halfway there and looked through the viewfinder. You couldn't see much. It wasn't going to be a good picture. I was too far away. It looked like a picture of a wooden deck with some pink on it. I would have to say hi and talk to her. I walked up to her and said hi, trying to sound as natural as I could.

"Oh, God, no, not for the yearbook," she said. "I look disgusting! Promise me you aren't going to take any."

She was slathered-up looking in the sun, but it had turned to a coat of oil instead of like the whipped Crisco look my sister had. "Just one, maybe," I said.

"Nope."

"What if it wasn't for the yearbook?" I asked.

"For what then?" she said.

"For… uh, me," I said.

"You want a picture of me looking ugly and greasy?"

"Yuh."

"Help yourself," she said, sitting up and flashing a great

29

smile.

"Really?" I asked. "Thank you," I said after I snapped it. I turned to walk away.

"Where are you off to?" she asked. "Don't you talk?"

"Handball court," I said. "Wanna come by in about fifteen minutes?"

"Maybe," she said, stretching out on her towel, much as I first saw her.

"Do you want a copy of the picture?" I asked. "I could get you one."

"I don't know. Probably not," she said, closing her eyes and resuming her tanning.

I walked along the beach, taking off my sandals and heard footsteps approaching me. I turned and much to my surprise, it was Caitlin Murphy, looking her skinny and tall self in a red swim-team Speedo suit, with a towel wrapped around the bottom of it. I didn't know she was on the BayWay swim team.

"Hey," she said.

"Hey," I said. "I didn't know you were on the team."

"Yeah," she said, rolling her eyes and then looking like she was going to blush. "An hour and a half a day." We walked some in silence. "We versus other clubs. Where are you heading?"

"Handball court," I said, for lack of any other answer.

"What's there?"

"Connor and Gary. We play Smash," I said.

"What's Smash?"

"It's a little like handball, but we use tennis racquets and try to hit the other guy on the rebound," I explained.

"Sounds violent," she said. "Can I come?"

I was surprised, but said yes. This was cool, but it still felt like she might bolt at any moment saying, "Nah, never mind."

Only she didn't.

She watched Gary and I play a round first, then Connor and me. She learned the rules and that if your serve went out you got penalized by having the other guy wing a ball at you as hard as he could while you stood with your hands up against the wall. There were no points involved with this, just pain.

Midway through the next round – Connor versus me again – she said she wanted to play the winner. That gave me extra incentive, and I smashed Connor 15-7 in record time.

It was me versus Caitlin now and the first thing she did was to slip out of her towel, folding it and putting it on the grass. I took off my windbreaker and lay my Beseler on top of it. It was her in her red Speedo and me in my turquoise Hawaiian bathing suit, no rules – well, there were rules – and the sun beat down on us without stop. I was sweating, and I was distracted. I missed shots I would've gotten if it were Gary doing it, and not because I was trying. It was more competitive than I thought it would be. Then, at 6-5 me, it happened; her serve went out. I got to throw a ball at her.

She walked up to the wall slowly, scrunching up her face like "Do I have to?" and then doing her thing of looking down and getting ready to blush, like a bad girl about to be punished – by *me*.

She put her hands up on the wall and exhaled.

"Higher," I shouted.

Caitlin moved her hands up higher and wider, leaning in towards the wall more and in a moment I will never forget spreading her legs more (for balance?), turning to look back at me and asking, "Like this?"

"Yes," I shouted, holding the tennis ball in my right hand, rubbing the felt with my thumb, looking for the seam.

She faced the wall. Then turned her head to look back at me and – I swear this – pushing her hips slightly back, her fine rear jutting upward toward me.

"Yes," I said again. "Like that."

"Nail her with it!" Connor shouted. "No mercy."

"Let it wail. You can't favor her because she's a girl," Gary added.

Caitlin waited for it, turning her head just a half inch to the left.

I squeezed the ball twice and knew what to do.

"Quit being a mama's boy," Connor offered.

She braced for impact.

No one expected the soft, underhand lob. It held its arc up into the sky, almost suspended in time, slowly descending in the direction of the top of her head, where it hit the back of it so gently that instead of bouncing off, it trailed down the back of her neck, between her shoulders, before slowly rolling down the line of her back vertebrae and tracing the fabric of her Speedo as it divided her lower back and rolled slowly lower. The ball fell to the ground and came rolling back in my direction after lingering on her for a magic moment.

Connor and Gary were temporarily speechless and Caitlin looked back at me, her back still arched, with a smile, and her beginning of a blush that was completely playful and alive.

I scooped the ball up, went over to the side and picked up her towel, my Beseler Topcon Super D, and my windbreaker, and said, "Let's go."

"Where are you going?" Gary asked.

"Not sure," I said, Caitlin falling in line next to me as I handed her the towel. I left my windbreaker off, and she carried her towel. "Exploring."

"That ball is ours," Connor shouted as we walked away.

Caitlin gave me a quick kiss on the shoulder. A kiss!

"I don't think so," I said. "There's lots of spare ones around."

I walked away with the ball. I kept it for a very long time.

Quiet Arms

Allegro ma non troppo

\#

Mrs. Lillian Ketcham seemed to be the oldest person in my life – somehow older than my grandparents, even though that couldn't be true. She was a different kind of old; unlike my immigrant grandparents, she was classy by Americanized English-Empire standards. There was an official quality to her love of classical stuff. This was real music, not like the *Pink Panther* theme song or Herb Alpert, Frank Sinatra, or The Beatles.

It was Clementi, Mozart, Chopin, and her true love, the one she really wanted me to encounter, the German: Beethoven. Beethoven, with his fiery sadness and anger. She talked about these people the way my dad talked about Al Sposato and other poker playing buddies, or guys he knew from the firehouse across the street from his pharmacy.

Getting yelled at as a fourteen-year-old by an old lady who had blue-tinted white hair no less, was totally different than getting yelled at as a nine-year-old. The fact that my *parents paid* her to yell at me made things way worse.

It enlarged my universe of people whom I wanted to scream back at, walk out on, and tell to leave me alone even larger and more unmanageable.

It was making me sick that this involved the piano, because it wasn't the piano that I hated. It was being constantly controlled and told what to do and when to do it that I hated.

My discovery, in first grade, that what I'd thought was a big piece of furniture in my classroom wasn't furniture at all, but something whose cover could be lifted up, exposing eighty-eight separate sculpted keys – some of them white, some of them black, some of them touched and pressed down, *while singing* – had me in awe. Whatever it was she was doing, I wanted in on that. I wanted to do it, too. By myself.

But now, just a handful of years later, I was sitting there, shoulders tense, hunched forward, stomach hurting, trying to make sense of the yelling, enduring it, waiting for it to end, but most of all waiting for it to make sense.

Mrs. Ketcham's skin looked like parchment with some purple areas on it. I'd seen my share of monster movies and skin like that looked more than a little like that of *The Mummy*. She moved as if her hips were locked in place and ratcheted to her lower back to make sure that she moved from room to room in one piece. She smelled like lilac perfume over oldness.

This was very different from the smell of my mother, with her Guerlain or my Aunt Lucille who wore bright red, shiny lipstick and Tabu. Mrs. Ketcham's blue-tinted white hair was pulled back in a bun and told the world that she meant business. The business was piano technique. Technique was the challenge, technique was the battleground, and childhood and adolescence was to some extent the enemy. Technique would prevail.

There was middle C, there were scales, both ascending and descending, hands separately, then hands together, there were arpeggios, there was *Teaching Little Fingers to Play* by John Thompson. I often wondered if Mrs. Ketcham read that as "Teaching Little Fingers to Fall Into Line On Command and March." There was a small book of staff paper with "Every Good Boy Does Fine" and "Good Boys Do Fine Always" written in her handwriting below large ovals on the staff.

Then there was her small dish of candy. After the battle – at the end of the lesson – no matter how off the mark it might've been, she would hold it out and prescribe how many you could take. "Go ahead, take one," meant it had been truly terrible; "Choose two," was better, but "Take a few" meant you were rising in the ranks of piano excellence faster than anyone could measure.

After a particularly successful go-round of a Clementi sonatina one day she asked me, "Do you know there is a black man working at the bank on Main Street as a teller?" I said no, I didn't know that, and she said, "And he's *perfectly nice*. He's a perfectly nice man."

I was thirteen, turning fourteen, and this was the same year James Brown recorded "Say It Loud – I'm Black and I'm Proud." I suddenly felt like Mrs. Ketcham was a personal friend of Mozart's, telling me that a wild African had been spotted running around Salzburg in the 1760s.

Then I realized that her point was not one of disapproval at the thought of this change to our little white home town – a black man working in the biggest bank on Main Street. What was next, a Russian in the Italian ice stand? – but the larger point: She was a very worldly, broad-minded person, unlike so many here. I mean, she hadn't run out of the bank screaming in horror or anything like that. She'd even touched money that he'd touched. I got that this was a huge thing for her.

"Try the Mozart again," she said, snapping me back to the present. "Slowly."

I started.

"Quiet arms!" Mrs. Ketcham shouted pointedly. "Quiet arms!"

This wasn't the second time, or the tenth time, or the twentieth time she'd do this. And each time she'd yell this phrase at me, I didn't know what she meant. Were my arms, somehow "too quiet"? Or they were too noisy, and supposed to get "quieter"? I didn't hear my arms making any noise in the first place – I always experienced my arms as silent – just my fingers maybe made some noise, as they existed as part of my hands, below the wrist, which was attached to my arms, which either became suddenly noisy to her or were not noisy enough? Whatever it was she was saying, or wanting, about my arms and their volume wasn't clear and I never, ever asked her what she was talking about.

"Quiet arms!" she yelled louder.

I did what I'd learned to do, which was somehow make some kind of micro-adjustment to my elbows, bringing them in closer to my body and making my playing slower and more deliberate. Though it was still unclear to me what I exactly was doing, or why it seemed to result in an end to the yelling. Each time I did it, I wasn't sure I could ever duplicate it again.

But this day was different. She said it again, even after my move. sounding like a bird now – an Old Bird. As if this Old Bird had only one phrase to describe everything: a worm, a sunrise, a hawk, an airplane: "Quiet arms!"

She let it drop, but looked annoyed.

My cagey attempts to provide written authentic-looking but largely fake weekly practice logs, written in marble notebooks my mother bought me at Kay's Stationary didn't seem to get her to let up on me. This became yet another ritual I had to do for Mrs. Ketcham. I was supposedly keeping track of exactly when my practicing began and ended each time. I knew it looked too easy and fake to say "7:45 pm to 8:30 p.m., Tuesday," so I would always make it something like "7:43 p.m. to 8:32 p.m., Tuesday," sure that the accuracy could no longer be questioned. It's not like I didn't practice; I did. Just not her way, nor in her amount of time.

I loved piano, but I hated Mozart. He'd been some sort of stupid little piano prodigy – the kind of kid you'd hate by the time he was eight – who'd pleased every adult whom he came into contact with. He was a show off of the worst sort, who'd whip off scales and arpeggios for no other reason than they went with the major key he was composing in, and he knew how to play these things fast. He had to sit on telephone books, or whatever they had back in the days of his little Austrian ass-kissing recitals, just to reach the keyboard. His hair – judging by the book I was playing from – was like a midget George Washington's, and the more I struggled to care about playing his music the more I wanted to punch him.

He'd be the smartest kid in the class, the one the teacher always called on, the one to bring the lunch and milk money in envelopes down to the main office because he was so very special and trusted. He would tell the teacher she looked particularly lovely today in the color blue she was wearing. Mozart was a little bitch, and I wanted to beat him up. Not that I ever really wanted to beat up people. But I'd make an exception for him.

Mozart had far less talent than Bob Dylan, I thought, and that was saying something. Dylan had shown us all that he could *not* sing, play guitar, and harmonica all at once. I guess he was a writer and that was enough.

Here was the big secret Mrs. Ketcham didn't know; here is what I didn't tell her; the thing that almost no one knew: I was in a rock band.

II. Andante molto mosso

On most days I came home and listened to music alone, mostly via Scott Muni, the gravel-voiced disc jockey on WNEW-FM. I alternated this with my father's record collection and the "Morning Mayor" of WABC-AM radio, Harry Harrison, for whatever pop music was happening. My heart, brain, and pelvis were being bombarded daily by music that lived on the loud barely-controlled edge of expression, sounding as different from Mozart as the Atlantic Ocean was from the little backyard plastic pool filled with hose water each summer. My memory bank became saturated with the straining sounds of Farfisa organs, the unrelenting energy of The Beatles, their more dangerous competitors, The Rolling Stones, the sounds of Hammond organs (The Young Rascals, Vanilla Fudge), the unimaginable perfection of "Disraeli Gears," and the mind-exploding dimensions of Jimi Hendrix.

I wasn't able to hold off on joining a band anymore. I set out to find a Farfisa organ to play because they were portable, could be blasted through an amplifier loudly, and looked cool. Some of them had white keys that were gray or black, while the black keys were white. They had a cool vibrato button that made everything sound psychedelic when you wanted it to, and the volume was controlled by a paddle above your right knee. Spreading your legs made it louder. I bought my Farfisa from a kid who was going to college for $170 (money I'd earned working part-time at my father's pharmacy). It was perfect, except for one leg that wobbled a little.

My earliest attempts to join the ranks of the musicians I admired found me learning the chords to Dylan's "Like a Rolling Stone," while a fellow thirteen-year-old guitar player bleated out about *feeling all alone*. We followed this up with our versions of "In the Midnight Hour" and "Knock on Wood." When we got to the lyrics got to the part about *doing things* in the midnight hour, I wasn't sure what they talking about it, but it sounded really good and dirty and against the rules, and that was more than good enough for me, especially for when we had a bass player and a drummer.

We weren't terrible. Well, sometimes we were terrible. But not all the time. Plus we were amplified.

But in this moment, my mind was obviously drifting, Mrs. Ketcham on my left, my elbows were wiggling, my fingers were chomping around, mangling some scales, and then mangling some piece I'd been assigned and Mrs. Ketcham had enough.

"All right, just stop," she said.

We sat there in silence, which sounded great. The moment, to me, felt like she was deciding whether or not to slap me, but that might've been reading too much into it. Instead we worked the piece hands separately, very slowly, and I started getting it.

Another week survived.

I rode home on my bike and was met by my mother asking how the lesson went and then declaring, "Thursday is garbage day. That means taking the cans out on Wednesday night. Don't forget. That's tomorrow night. This is your job. We don't want to have to keep reminding you."

The next day, late afternoon my mother walked into the kitchen while I was snacking on Cheetos and reminded me that the garbage cans had to be taken out that night. I bristled, upset. "I'm *going to, okay*? Just stop lecturing me."

"I'm not lecturing, I'm reminding you. I thought you needed a reminder."

"I already told you, *I don't want a reminder*."

"All right, then, we'll stop reminding you. Just do it."

"I already *said* I'd do it."

"Well when, then? It's already Wednesday night!"

I went up upstairs to my room and turned on music – loudly at first, before turning it down some – through the integrated phono/FM/AM radio component set I'd gotten for my bar mitzvah. Putting on AM radio these days only got you songs like "Honey," by Bobby Goldsboro or "Tighten Up," by Archie Bell and the Drells. Switching to FM got you "Mrs. Robinson," and Donovan's "Hurdy Gurdy Man" – the creepiest song I'd yet let into my fifteen-year-old consciousness. I didn't know what it was about, but I knew if I ever figured out what a Hurdy Gurdy Man was or did, you should run away from him fast. My favorite FM song, however (soon to make the switch to AM) was The Doors' "Hello, I Love You." It was only about three or four chords, but it had an incredibly buzzy, nasal organ sound that clicked with something insistent in my own head when it came to girls.

I thought about the lyrics a lot. How could you love someone before you knew their name? How could that be? I knew the names of all the girls in my school, and in some ways had been studying them since third grade. Sometimes I'd choose one of their names and would see what their initials looked with mine together, with a heart drawn around it. I knew some girls, and their names from Bay Shore and East Islip, too. I guess the love without names thing was how older kids operated? Was this a hippie thing? You just saw someone and loved them? Was this just about sex?

I thought about Mrs. Ketcham. Not only was I cheating on her and Mozart by lying about my practice habits, I was cheating on them both another way: There were others in my world on TV.

III. Allegretto

I came downstairs and watched *I Dream of Jeannie*. I couldn't believe my good fortune, there was actually a show on TV about a sexy blonde woman in harem pants and a red bra, and sometimes just in a man's shirt, who called the guy in the show "Master," smiled all the time, and who would do *whatever* he asked her to do. This was the best show ever. Better than *The Man From U.N.C.L.E* and even *Combat*. Second runner up was *Bewitched*, which featured a cute tall blonde woman with magical witch powers who never behaved the way that ordinary married women were supposed to. Even though she wouldn't do whatever the man in the show wanted her to do, you could tell she really loved him, anyway. She always had a special smile for him, even if it was a naughty one. Maybe she did whatever he wanted her to after the cameras weren't rolling.

I knew I had to practice piano that Wednesday night, after watching Jeannie and Samantha and imagining myself in their worlds, alone with them, just getting to know each other, and the TV was in the same room as the piano, so my practicing meant my sister Jody couldn't watch anything while I was doing it.

"How come I have to miss Carol Burnett just because he has to practice?" she'd ask.

"Because it's *culture*," I spat out. "You should try it."

"It's unfortunate, but that's the way it is," my mother said, after my sister appealed to her. I shot my sister a fast look of triumph.

I sat at the piano and started playing the Czerny exercises. Boring, boring, boring.

My mind wandered, as my fingers flew up and down the keyboard like a machine. I couldn't believe anyone would write music like this and call it music. Gradually I could play it faster.

So what?

I tried the scales Mrs. Ketcham had given me to practice. Played, repeated, played. Played, repeated, played. I realized I could do them faster now. I went on to the arpeggios. Yup.

I would call Steve and Gary and our band would practice this Saturday. All day Saturday. It was time for us to get really good.

We'd get to play dances. Maybe even CYO dances where the Catholic girls were said to be wild.

Aunt Rose and the
Instamatic

# #

Our band needed a name. It couldn't be just Steve and me and Gary and whoever was hanging around on Saturdays downstairs at my newly refinished (with cool fake wood paneling) basement. We needed an identity, and band names were getting wilder. It had to have the word "The" in it. But animal names seemed to be an old thing by now: The Beatles, The Monkees, Rhinoceros ... they weren't original anymore. Question Mark and the Mysterians were pretty hard to live up to, as was Moby Grape, The Troggs, and The Strawberry Alarm Clock. Some of the other Long Island and Jersey bands that were making it had names I thought were stupid, like The Young Rascals and Vanilla Fudge. We couldn't come up with anything for a name.

Sitting around debating names with my group always felt cool, relaxed and easy. This was us *before* we got famous, I thought. These moments would be memorable. Lessons with Mrs. Ketcham now were the exact opposite.

Midway through this week's mechanical clanking noise/mess of whatever the under-practicing offering was, she stopped me. She was going to make this exactly as uncomfortable for me as she'd decided she needed to. "Did you practice?" she asked, looking into my face in profile.

"Yes," I lied, staring straight ahead. "Some."

She didn't say anything.

"I could have practiced more."

She seemed to choose her words carefully. "This isn't fair."

I started to choke back feelings; even though I couldn't identify them, they were coming out as tears. I gulped them back.

"To yourself, to me, or to your parents who pay for this," she said, bringing forth the full blush of shame and guilt in me that she'd been fishing for. I finally could gulp them back no more and burst into tears. Me, the talented, ashamed, sorry, guilty boy sitting with Mrs. Ketcham, the first woman other than my mother to bring my intimate feelings into the open with full-bodied expression. I hated it, I hated this moment, and – for the time being – I hated her. Why couldn't she just leave me alone?

I sniveled my way through the rest of the hour together, got offered two candies anyway – I guess crying got you one for a consolation prize – and I swung my backpack over my shoulder and hopped onto my bicycle to ride home. I took some consolation in riding over the big hill on South Bay Avenue, giving me tons of momentum and miles per hour as I cruised towards Wave Crest, Avondale, and Shebar Drive.

At my next lesson, I was doing my best to forcefully make my fingers move to the next place, no feeling, no connection, all show when Mrs. Ketcham leaned forward. "All right, stop!" She had an idea, she said. "I know what would work for you," she said. "Duets." And she stood up, stiffly walked to her special cabinet, rummaged around and came back with a *Four Hands Duets* book. "I have just the person for you to call. She would be a capable partner for you, for this work."

She spread the music book out before me, pointed at me to play the high melody parts and she moved to sit next to me on the bench. She would play the supporting bass hands. I'd never sat so close to Mrs. Ketcham before.

The song rang out beautifully. It sounded like six piano players were playing at once. It was kind of exciting.

It was power.

It being the second week of December, as we ended the lesson she gave me three candies and said, "It's Chanukah for you people, now, right? Unless I've gotten it wrong." She had gotten it right, and she added as a coda, "It's terrible how much you people have suffered." She paused and gave this some more thought. "I've always admired your people's determination and ways with money. I have just the person for you to call. She would be a capable partner for you, for this work."

The suggestion she made then was that Ruth Finklestein and I pair up as piano duet Masters because we were both members of the "you-people" crowd. And of course, because Ruth could play with less noisy arms than I did, I guess.

Ruth Finklestein: fellow member of our nearly vanished grandparents' European tribe, was no Jeannie or even Samantha. She was like a young version of one of my grandmother's sisters, I thought; what Aunt Eva might've looked like had I been teamed up with her to play duets in 1930, just before the Germans invaded. We'd have to forge passports or something and flee to America if we were lucky enough to not meet the fate of the rest of the family.

I couldn't imagine Aunt Eva in harem pants and a red bra.

I called Ruth. "Hi."

"Hi," she said in a neutral voice.

"So ... I guess we're doing this?" I asked, trying to match her neutrality. (I had to wonder what Mrs. Ketcham had told her all about me. Ruth seemed already competitive with me; maybe she'd been told I was a little more advanced on piano than she was?) We agreed to practice on Saturday at 2 p.m.

at her house. We'd both been practicing our parts, and they were easy.

I rode my bike over that Saturday, hopping off and leaning it against a tree in her yard. I rang the doorbell. Her mother answered the door. She didn't look like my mother at all. My mother was kind of sleek, with arched eyebrows and angular cheeks, kind of like some of the actresses in the black-and-white movies of the '50s. Ruth's mother was shorter, chubbier, and looked like a much more practical mother than mine.

"She's upstairs, getting ready. But you can come in. Come right in," she said, ushering me into a living room that seemed to be already occupied by three old people sitting on a plastic-slip covered sofa. "This is Ruth's Grandma Sophie, my mother, and Grandpa Jack." They both waved at me, murmuring little hellos. "And that is Rose, Sophie's sister, my aunt." Rose just stared at me.

What was this? A United Jewish Appeal meeting? No sooner did Grandma Sophie and Grandpa Jack smile and wave at me than Aunt Rose brought her small camera to her face, snapping a fast one of me entering the room. The Kodak Instamatic Flash Cube blinded me as Ruth entered.

"Isn't this just…?"

"Practice?" Ruth finished the question for me. "Yeah."

"So…"

"I told them not to watch," she whispered. "They wouldn't listen."

We sat down to her Story & Clark spinet piano, her taking the upper octaves and me the lower ones, and we could feel her relatives staring at our back. The room lit with another flash and I counted off, "One-two-three-four…"

We sounded surprisingly good. It sounded like two pianos. We banged out the four-handed piece in perfect unison, filling the two levels of the suburban house with ease. Ruth and I sat on the bench almost touching, me slamming away at the bass chords, she taking the melody. I loved the rumbling of the bass and how the notes would linger even after the melody went elsewhere. I made sure I was a little louder than she was.

The flash on Aunt Rose's camera went off two more times. We could hear them behind us, talking about whether you needed to change the flash every time you used it; Aunt Rose had trouble understanding that the Instamatic flashcube, as it rotated on the square, allowed for four shots before you had to do anything like pop it off and put a new one on. Grandpa Jack was worried that you had to focus the camera "So you don't get the blur," and someone was patiently explaining you didn't need to do anything.

I knew what the old people behind us were thinking. This was the antidote to the holocaust; if Sharon and I got married and had eight children they could say, "Hey, Hitler, take a look at *this*; ten American Jews in a happy family. How do you like that?"

And all I could think of was that if Ruth and I got married and had eight children – even four! – there'd be endless trips for allergy shots, baseball games, dance rehearsals, and more piano lessons.

Even sitting there, playing, I knew I wasn't going to be responsible for attempting to respond to the holocaust through duets then marriage. Uh-uh.

"Again!" Aunt Rose shouted. I looked at Ruth, and she shrugged her left shoulder, so we did it again. I counted off, this time, boldly starting with only "Two, three, four..." We played louder and bolder than before, once again hitting all the marks. The piano seemed to expand, as if it were proud of itself; a horse with the two of us riding it, going fast.

The slip-covered crowd roared and clapped, and Grandpa Jack asked us to pose in front of the piano. We stood there stiffly, nice kids, both of us, shoulders almost touching, both of us holding in our right hands books of sheet music, our left hands not knowing what to do, our smiles big and forced, trying to give them what they wanted, and I wanted out of there so badly I would've pushed Grandma Sophie out of the way to hop on my bike if this didn't end in thirty seconds.

We finished up and it turned out they had pastries for us set out, as if this were an engagement party. I left as soon as a nice boy could decently do so.

I would not call Ruth again. I would not write to her. I would not again play the four-handed holocaust antidote her European survivor family longed to hear. And while one school of thought was that the best form of revenge was for my people to find each other and multiply, another school of American thought was that the best revenge was to finally be left alone, to make ordinary American decisions to do whatever we wanted to, with whomever we wanted to.

My people – the American newcomers – were risky and wise and the part of my people who stayed behind – the ones who believed they were Polish or Ukrainian – the ones who were all in on bets that the warm hearts of their Christian neighbors would protect them from the storm of bullets and ditches and poison gas – well, they were all dead.

I was starting to understand that being a young American, to me, meant not being tied to the murders and disasters of twenty-two years ago. I wouldn't be tied a murderous past. These things were surely over now. I mean, it was 1968.

I zipped home, put my bike in the garage, went upstairs without saying hello to anyone and put on my Steppenwolf album, "Born to be Wild." It couldn't get loud enough for me.

Ladies and Gentlemen, The Beatles (Part 2)

# #

"Want to blow off some bottle rockets?" Gary asked with a glint in his eye.

"Where?"

"Down the road at the end of St. Mark's, where's it's marked 'Private,'" he ventured.

"Yeah. What if we get caught?" I asked.

"We're kids. We won't get caught," he said, laughing.

We both tried to ignore our boners, which slowly melted away and allowed us to move freely once the magazine was put away and the bottle rockets, cherry bombs, and M-80s produced. *Boners were like magic, too*, I thought. They didn't respond to logic and there was nothing fake about them. They were part of the universe that made you wanna.

They had warned us in third, fourth, and fifth grade about playing with fireworks, about the kid in Setauket who put his eye out playing with a bottle rocket, about the kid who blew off his finger in Connecticut. This was interesting, but had nothing to do with us. Gary and I would be careful. We were raised that way.

We finished the beers – which somehow tasted even worse than before – and we peed on his next-door neighbors' side yard, chuckling quietly in the dark. Then we gathered everything into a little backpack that Gary would wear. We were careful to move quietly, zipping up the tent behind us and pointing the flashlight down. It didn't matter really, because Sherry and Barry were at it now, yelling loudly inside the house about something. Gary's brother was sleeping over someone else's house this weekend, so aside from his sister, who was home from college but basically almost never home, his parents had the run of the house in terms of throwing things and screaming. It didn't occur to either of us that his sister would come home in the middle of it.

It was the perfect temperature for sneaking around; there was some gathering summer dew on the grass, and it wasn't so hot that it was oppressive. Gary took out his old Sting Ray bike from the garage and his brother's clunky three-speed Schwinn, which I got to ride and we headed off toward Sherwood Elementary School, where we'd dutifully spent five years of our lives leaning subtraction, something about New York State, and sentence structure. We could almost diagram a sentence but we were years away from writing one that mattered.

This was a perfect place to test the bottle rockets. Just riding our bikes up over the curb in the middle of the night, banging them up hard over the sidewalk instead of taking the ramp, felt like a tremendous, exciting violation of the rules. Playing with matches and shooting something off in the playground would be even better. Gary produced a few small firecrackers when we stopped riding, standing there with the bikes between our legs, and he quickly lit three of them and threw them. It was a great sharp snapping sound, puncturing the night.

The end of St. Mark's Lane was the snooty part of town. Old people, station wagons, big front lawns, and lots of gates and fences. We set the M-80s up on the big fence that separated the regular part of town from the so-so-special part of town, arranging the remaining barrage of bottle rockets and cherry bombs so they leaned up against the lowest rungs of the fence, aimed at enemy territory.

We threw the bikes down and crouched. There was the question of which to light first. We decided on me lighting the bottle rockets (very fast fuses) and Gary lighting the cherry bombs (medium fuse), and M-80s (supposedly a three-second fuse). That was enough time to hop on our bikes and get accelerated in some direction away from the action as they all exploded and shot into the sky at once.

It would be like the parts of the James Bond movies where the person calmly walks away from something that massively explodes in a fireball right behind them, as they continue walking, maybe saying something funny. Only it'd be us on our bikes. I'd just have to think of some witty remark.

There were no cars, no sounds really. I thought I heard a squirrel or something rushing off behind a tree.

"Okay, no second chances," Gary said pointedly. I nodded. "As soon as yours are lit, one second, I light mine, boom, we're off on bikes."

Here's the amazing part. That's just how it happened. We leaned over the explosives like trained professionals, locked eyes, didn't even say, "Do it," just nodded, and I lit the first match. I brought the hot head of the flame to the tail of the bottle rocket fuse, keeping it a minute distance away, watching the fuse somehow suck the flame up into itself, sizzling with mean promise, one, two, three bottle rockets lit, then hearing Gary lighting the matches and moving it to the cherry bombs and M-80s.

The explosion – a series of explosions, really – were the loudest things we'd ever heard in our town in all of our years there. It was just like a sudden Russian artillery bombardment of Coach Cuticelli's Lane at the same time as a Grumman Hellcat F6F strafed it from the other side of the horizon. The booming explosions shook the mailboxes around us, even though we were already on our bikes and considerably past the blast site.

You could practically hear jet-fighters zooming past their targets, confirming their direct hits to base. "Far f'ing out!" Gary exclaimed. It wasn't just that the explosions were loud; it was that they were shaking, however briefly, everything that normally didn't shake. Horseshoes on barns, decorations on doors and apparently the insides of dogs' sleeping brains. Because they erupted in crazy fury, from all different sides of St. Mark's Lane, of Bay Third Street, even as far away as Bayberry Lane. They howled in alarm, screamed, and barked ferociously, like the under-rehearsed sixth-grade chorus we were stuck in all year. Their message to their owners was stark and immediate: "Something's wrong! We are under attack! Take cover! We are under attack!"

Lights started going on in houses and we were riding the bikes faster than anyone could see us or place us at the scene, we thought, which to us meant faster than the speed of light. The combination of the dogs' fearful warnings and the lights popping on must've added fifteen miles per hour to our bicycle acceleration as well as to our deep sense of accomplishment.

We leaned right on our bikes and accelerated at warp speed, knowing that it was mission accomplished. The sounds of our pedals pumping was matched by our heavy breathing as we accelerated.

We jumped off the bikes back at Gary's house and leaned them against the maple tree in the side of the yard. We decided to come into the house to make post-attack nighttime sandwiches, flush with our success, ready to stay awake til dawn. The sandwiches would have to be very particular and very right. Pickles would be good, too.

Much to our surprise Gary's sister, Penny, was sitting in

the living room, leaning forward on the edge of the hassock, then backwards on it, as she listened to their mother Sherry's slightly-slurred, dramatic speech. Sherry was sitting in the big stuffed chair, holding a drink in her left hand and a lit cigarette in her right.

"This *is my* house and as long as you are sleeping here, you have to play by my rules. College or no college," Sherry said, drawing the cigarette to her mouth and slowly taking a drag. "I couldn't sleep, I was so worried, I had to take a Valium." She took a sip of her drink.

"What about Dad?" asked Penny.

"Huh?" Sherry asked.

"I said, 'What about Dad?' *It's his* home, too, isn't it? And where, like, *is he*?" Penny spat.

"That has nothing to do with nothing. Dad ... me ... we're *adults*. And you *respect adults*."

"So he's nowhere to be found, Mom?" Penny shot back. "Again?"

"Your Dad *has his* life, I *have my* life. When you get older, you'll *have your* life."

"I already have a life," Penny said. Then, whirling to look at us, she said, "What are these two little freaks doing here?"

Sherry turned to stare at us as if she were noticing us for the first time. "She has a point," she said. "The girl has a point. What are the two of you doing up? You need your sleep. Teenagers need extra sleep."

"We're camping out, out front," Gary offered.

"Probably drinking and playing with themselves," Penny offered, trying to sidle up to her mother before she remembered her mother had been yelling at her.

"*No,*" Gary protested.

"Oh... what... you've been studying for the PSATs?" his

sister asked, sneering.

"Where were *you*?" Gary fired back.

"In older teenager-land," Penny said immediately. "Deal with it. How are things in the sandbox? Did you lose your pacifier or babysitter somewhere?"

"You were the babysitter. So yeah, you got lost," Gary said, thinking it sounded meaner than it did.

"I moved on to bigger and better things, twerp."

"Then why are you here?" he asked.

"Just get out of here, you spaz! Mom and I are trying to talk!" she yelled.

"Girl talk," Sherry said. "Mom-girl talk."

"Are you pregnant?" Gary asked.

"No! Get *out of here!*" Penny said, grabbing at the Sears catalog on the table in front her and throwing it full force at her brother's head.

He was able to knock it to the side, but not before it knicked his head with one of its square edges. He played the injury up immediately, saying, "Owww, owww,*owww*! *Mom*? Did you see that? Mom, she's psycho! Maybe it's *drugs*! She and her Commie friends."

"Get out!" Penny now stood and screamed. Sherry sipped her drink.

"She's like that aggressive dog that Uncle Al had at the boathouse. Psycho!" Gary taunted.

Sherry spoke with a hushed, slurry voice. "Maybe it's best if the two of you boys find something to do. A board game. You have a lot of board games. We bought you them. Many times. Wait? Isn't it *night*? It's night! Just go to sleep. It'll all look better in the morning."

"What will?" Gary asked. "This family?"

"Oh, now *that* is beyond the pale," Sherry said, shaking her head. "There's no call for that. There are kids out there who don't even *have* families. Disadvantaged kids. You *have* a family. You should be grateful."

"I am. I am full of great about it, Mom. But right now I have to go upstairs and find a Band-Aid to patch up where Penny hit me in the head with whatever she threw. So please excuse us," he said, signaling me to rise and follow him.

Penny searched around really fast and grabbed the smaller Fingerhut catalog and threw it at him, harder than before. This one bounced off Gary's back.

You could see where the catalog bounced off of his face because it was all red, but there wasn't any blood, so I didn't get why we were walking upstairs to the bathroom for a Band-Aid. We walked in together; the shower curtain was of bright blue, green, and yellow tropical fish, and it was the kind that had a layer of plastic behind the plastic to make it look more real or textured or something.

Years later, I realized it was just to keep the water in the tub. Gary's mother always had these little carved soaps instead of the yellow Dial soap that my house had; there was one of a swan, another one of a starfish, and one of a seashell. I didn't get how you'd use the swan for soap without breaking its head off. Maybe if you were really delicate, I thought, you could just rub the swan against you and you'd get delicately clean. Or you could break its neck.

"Check this out," Gary said, sinking to his knees, opening the cabinet door beneath the sink and fumbling around before emerging with a long cylinder of wrapped white paper. "You know what this is?" he asked.

"Candle?" I ventured.

"No."

"Barbeque lighter?" I was grasping. I'd seen things that were pointy that could light things without matches.

"It's a tampon," Gary said, with authority. "You know

where it goes?"

I didn't.

He started nodding, slowly. "Yeah. Up *there*."

"Up…"

"Yeah," he said, still nodding. "There."

"Wh…"

"Once a month," he advised, sounding like a doctor on TV.

"It…"

"That's what they do. In secret. When they ask to go to the bathroom in school, during class, and the teachers give them those little looks, like, yeah, okay, you can go, but Gary and his friends can't? It's to put one of these up themselves."

"Is that to stop babies? From happening?" I asked.

He shook his head from side to side. "There's a lot you don't know," he said. "Maybe that's okay. So. .. we're going to take two of these… here you go; one for you, one for me ... and we're going to decorate before we go back downstairs."

I followed him into Penny's room. There was a Monkees poster on the wall above her bed. It was the picture in which they were trying to look tough. Davey and Mickey were standing in front, with tight pants on. Mickey had this cool red shirt with double sets of buttons on the front, his hands resting against his thighs, and Davey had the same kind of shirt on, only in blue. They weren't smiling. Behind them Peter and Mike stood. Mike, with his hands on his hips, looking like he wasn't entirely convinced about this band, Peter in a psychedelic shirt, with longer hair than the rest of them. The word "Monkees" blazed across Davey's pants in a guitar shape, right over where his dick was, with the other end of the guitar, where the red frets were, landing right over Mickey's dick. It was as if their dicks were connected by this red guitar. I'd never noticed that stuff before; it was clear which two guys the band belonged to.

Penny's room smelled like lemon and that was because she had a big thing of Love's Fresh Lemon Body Mist on the night table. The dispenser looked like a big bulbous yellow-headed dick. You could see the lemony liquid in the bottom half of it through see-through glass, though. It looked like she'd used a bunch of it.

"That's them trying to look like hoods," Gary said, pointing back at the Monkees poster. "What a joke. They're not even a band."

"They had as many hits as Herb Alpert and The Tijuana Brass," I said.

"And what? One-tenth as many as The Beatles? What about the Stones?" Gary asked, as he went over to Penny's dresser and started pulling open the top drawer. "They were put together by TV guys."

"I thought you didn't like the Beatles," I asked.

"'Revolver'? 'Violins?' 'And Your Bird Can Sing'? No, I don't like that," he said. "Do you?"

Actually, I didn't. My favorite album was still *Meet The Beatles*.

Gary was rustling around in the top drawer now.

"But the new one," he reflected, pulling out his prize and holding it up high to display from several viewing areas: a purple stretchy pair of Penny's panties. "'Sergeant Pepper's is *unreal*."

We stood quietly and considered the underpants. It was about 3 a.m. Okay, I'd be a liar if I said anything other than it made you want to. To see Penny in them. This was the next best thing.

Then I felt bad because it was Gary's sister. Even if he didn't.

"Do you want another pair? One of your own?" he

asked. "To take home? What color?"

I was speechless; I expected Penny to come barging in at any moment, to throw a cement block at his head or stab him with a machete. I listened for signs of that, but all I could hear was the muffled conversation of Sherry and her downstairs, punctuated by crying. I think it was Penny crying.

"Blue, black, or white?" Gary asked, as if we were at the Italian ice place with almost forty flavors.

"White," I whispered, and they were mine. He threw them to me, and I pocketed them.

"There's one thing I know," Gary said, carefully arranging the purple pair of panties on her pillow with the tampon leaning up against it, jutting out at a dick-like angle. "And that is you'll never hear anyone introduce them like, 'Ladies and gentlemen: The Monkees.' People would laugh. And they should. Some things are in a class by themselves."

I stood around not knowing what to do with the tampon I was still holding. "What about this?" I asked. "I don't really want it."

He took it from me and placed it in across the dial pad of her Princess phone in between the receiver and the handset.

"We didn't really get that sandwich, did we?" Gary asked as he led the way out of her room toward the downstairs and the kitchen.

"Aren't you supposed to have a Band-Aid on your face?" I asked.

"They won't notice. You'll see," he said, confidently.

We came downstairs and heard his mother wrapping things up after a long exhale of smoke. Penny had a tissue and was blowing her nose.

"It's men, Penny. Just men."

A Foot In The River
(Part 1)

# #

Age twelve: first base was the telephone pole. Third base was definitely the garbage cans in front of 5 Bay Third Street. We usually had some part of a cardboard box for home plate. Second base tended to float around some, particularly before our no-stealing rule and depending a lot on who was playing second. It made for some epic arguments, if not actual fights, particularly if Dick Decker was around. No one called him Dick ever. He was simply "Decker."

Decker always had firecrackers. He had those little things you could flick at kids that would make a sharp snapping sound. Like a portable mini-firecracker, just to remind you that he was all about things your family and your home had no idea of. He was right; I couldn't figure out where to buy the things. If you whipped them on the ground fast they made a truly wicked sound that made you jump. I tried both Kay's Stationary and Louie's Luncheonette, but I didn't really know what I was asking for: I had to act it out for them, and they both shook their heads and laughed. The guy in Louie's asked, "You mean caps? For cap guns? We have rolls of the regular ones and the plastic ones are on the wall." But that wasn't it. They weren't caps. Only Decker seemed to know, and no one was asking him. We were trying to stay out of his way.

Decker had matches on him, too. Having perfected the art of flicking things at people, he would demonstrate how he could light and flick a wood match pretty much at the same time. The demonstration, though, wasn't for educational purposes. There would be no goggles and lab classwork you'd have to fill in ("Can you see the chlorophyll?" "No." "What color is it?").

You observed Decker in action when he was trying to set you on fire. Which he said he wanted to do to me one month after my twelfth birthday as we stood about six feet apart from each other down by the fishing dock on Great South Bay. Steve and Gary and I usually went there with some old chicken parts or leftover meat from home, a flashlight, and a big crab net to try catch them. This day, for some reason, it was me, alone, leaning over the side, whispering to the crabs, "C'mon, baby, you know you want some. Mmmmmm-mmmmmm, good chicken guts and leftovers from Jody's plate and smelly stuff, c'mon you know you can't pass it up, these are like Dunkin' Donuts for crabs, just a little closer, uh-huh…C'mon, baby, you know you want it…'Take the last train to Clarksville…' "

Decker was suddenly there, laughing and staring at me. "Are you kidding me? Were you singing to a crab? Little baby wants his crabby?" I scrambled to my feet. "Do you know how far that puts you on the scale of faggotdom? You can't even measure it."

"It was working," I found my way to say, while scanning for an exit. He had it blocked. There was the water behind me and him in front of me, blocking the road. He had his – or someone's – Sting Ray bike leaning on its side next to him.

"Yeah? Was it going to kiss you?" he asked. He glared at me. I wondered about why he was always this way, why he was so mad. "You think I'm going to beat you up, don't you?" he asked.

I thought of three smart-ass things to say to him, but

didn't say any of them because yeah, I thought he was about to beat me up.

"I'm not going to do that," he said. "I'm going to burn you up." That's when he took out his matches and did his light-and-flick throwing trick, launching, one, two, three matches in a row at me. I didn't know much about matches, because we'd always been told to stay away from them.

I had just turned twelve and was raised to be a good boy. For all I knew you could burst out in flames if the lit matches touched you. Like the scenes they had in *Rescue 8*, the TV show where emergency responders raced to the scene of a car roll-over or terrible accident, dragging people out just before the whole thing went up in a ball of flames. I didn't want to go up in a ball of flames. I wanted to be home for dinner.

The first match landed at my feet. The second one went wide, to my left. I bolted, throwing the crab net in his direction and it must have deflected the incoming third match. At the same time I kicked the empty plastic bucket in his direction, like it was a soccer ball, grabbed the flashlight, and ran.

He was distracted by the movements and sound long enough to give me two whole seconds of lead time, and I got past him. I considered grabbing the bike and taking it as I ran past, but I was afraid he might launch a bazooka at me or something. I ran fast.

"Yeah, that's right, run away, little baby. Keep running. Run to your mommy, go suck her titties," he taunted. Decker's threats, remarks ,and sayings always had references to tits in them. He wouldn't stop talking about them. And never in a good way.

But that was back then. Four years later and I'd finally made it to age sixteen. We were sitting around the dinner table, my father looking tired and my mother looking vaguely annoyed. Dad lit his usual after-dinner cigarette as my mother cleared the table. *Only two more years of this*, I thought to myself.

"All I want is a house by the water," Dad said. "Nelson Simons bought this little place out in Shirley years ago. A shack. On the water. You know what that place is worth now?" he asked to whomever was listening.

I looked over and my sister was playing with her old Chatty Cathy, adjusting its clothing. She'd just turned twelve years old, but she liked to act younger and Chatty Cathy was a classic toy of hers. The string that you pulled to get Cathy to say stuff had broken years ago, and my sister accused me of having done it. Really it was that Chatty Cathy wasn't built for much wear, and she'd gone silent after too much time and string-pulling in our family.

"Do you know how much?" my father repeated.

"A lot," I said.

"Almost half a million dollars. He fixed it up, made little repairs here and there. Outdoor shower, fish-cleaning table. View of the Bay, bridge in the distance, ferries from Sayville ... year-round view," he said, sounding sad.

"Did Nelson have any kids?" I asked.

"No. Nelson never got married," he said.

"Well, there you go," I offered. "Without us, you might've had a chance."

My father looked angry. "That's not what I'm saying," he said. "I'm saying that he felt it and acted on it, even back then. What is it that the hippies are saying?"

"Turn on, tune, in, drop out?" I volunteered.

"No, not that."

"Today is the first day of the rest of your life?"

"No."

"Be here now?"

"No. He bought it then."

"But it was *now* back then when he bought it," I argued.

My father thought about it. "Maybe. But it was something else I heard."

"Follow your heart?" my mother offered, after he was done stubbing out the end of his cigarette in the remaining rice on the plate.

"What's that from?" he asked her.

"Oh, that book... the one about the seagull. Named Jonathan," my mother said.

My sister and I both laughed at the same time; she was spitting out some of her food, and I think some was even coming out of her nose as our laughter grew.

"What book is that?" I asked, setting her up some more.

"*Jonathan, The Seagull*, I think," she said. "It's very beautiful. But it's sad."

"Does he buy real estate on the bay like Nelson did by the end of the book?" I asked.

"All right, all right..." my father said, catching on, but also doing nothing about it.

"Why don't you read it?" my mother asked me,directly. "You used to love to read. Now all you is blast music."

"I read," I said. "Just not books written by seagulls."

"He didn't write it," my mother said, getting aggravated. "It's from his point of view."

"So he dictated it? You're sure it's not called *Jonathan Buys A Seagull* or *Jonathan Versus the Seagull*?" I asked.

"Follow your heart," my father repeated. "That's not it."

"'Love means never having to say you're sorry'?" I threw into consideration.

"No." My father seemed to be half enjoying this now.

"'You can never go home again'?" I asked.

"No. Something about a river." It seemed to be on the tip of his tongue now.

"A foot in the river? That one?" I asked.

"I don't know. Go do your homework. And your sister has her turn for the TV tonight; you had it last night," he informed us.

I called Gary; he told me he'd heard Decker got a fire extinguisher to explode, somehow, by hitting it with a sledgehammer enough times.

"Decker has a sister, you know. That and his parents explain why he is the way he is," Gary offered.

"Yeah? How's that?" I asked.

"Well, his sister is six years older than he is and kids older than us said she is out of control with sex. She says yes to anyone her age or up to four years younger."

"Anyone with a dick, you mean?" I clarified.

"Yes. Frank Parkin told us he was over Decker's house once and he heard his sister on the phone to someone saying, 'There's got to be a hundred miles of dick in this town and I can't get six inches.'"

We were both quiet for a minute. "Frank Parkin is not a reliable source," I said.

"Maybe not," Gary said, "But it doesn't sound like something Frank would make up, because it is a compound sentence."

"So how does that explain anything?"

"She walks around half-dressed all the time. Decker has been staring at tits and panties for years while the rest of us have been imagining them," Gary said. "And his mother's never home to cook anything. He eats cereal for dinner and sometimes a hot dog."

"How do you know any of this?" I asked.

"I got him talking instead of beating me up behind Burger King last year. I think we should invite him to hang out with us and play twilight baseball on Bay Third sometime."

I pondered this. We were old for it, but we still played. "But no flicking stuff that explodes or has fire, okay? And it has to be that we outnumber him and can cover for each other if he turns crazy."

"Of course we outnumber him," Gary said, calmly. "He'll probably be scared of us."

"I ain't scared of you little faggots," Decker said when he arrived for his first invitational play-til-it-gets-dark ballgame.

"The feeling is mutual," Gary said, settling in at shortstop, tossing the ball to first.

"And I don't know how long I'm staying," Decker offered.

"Stay as long as you can," Gary offered nicely. "You want to bat?"

It was weird seeing Decker so close up and not menacing. It was kind of like seeing Godzilla dressed up in a suit for his school picture.

We all paused to notice the old retired German doctor, Dr. Sharfenberger, strutting down St. Mark's Lane with his German Shepherd, Schnitzel. He kept a military pace, always had a walking stick, and didn't acknowledge anything around him. *He looked personally indignant at having lost World War II*, I thought.

Schnitzel matched his walk, his broad shoulders atop a strong, padded stride. We all knew Sharfenberger didn't like kids. The one time our baseball got wild and crossed over his approaching path, he ignored all of our calls to throw us the ball back and kept walking straight ahead. "Maybe he's deaf," Gary wondered.

The only way Decker would talk to us without being angry was to express his anger about someone, or something else, to us. During our seventh inning stretch break, he held forth.

"Did you see the tits on that substitute teacher in social studies?" he asked "Right there. A blind man could seed them. Or better yet, bump into them. Slowly…"

We murmured stupid things in response.

"She wanted us to see them. That's how messed up she is," he said.

This was complex stuff: the rules of tits. Having them, for a girl, was a must, and having great ones was fantastic, but showing them freely made you disgusting or bad. The key seemed to be in accepting that they were something we could steal our enjoyment of. We would take it; offering them was not the way this went. We were supposed to discover them and somehow get them. A girl being a girl who enjoyed them for herself was messed up. According to Gary, this made Decker really old-fashioned, even though he liked to sound like a rebel.

I faded on the conversation about Decker's second cousin's bra size when I saw that Lynne Dinunzo had come out of her front door onto her porch at 86 Bay Third Street, and was practicing skills with a yo-yo. It seemed like a pretty young-kid thing to be doing – after all, we'd all be driving in a few years. But there was Lynne, standing there in tight, white short-shorts, chewing gum, and working her yo-yo. Lynne wasn't beautiful the way Steffi Mendishack was, but in this summer moment, it all didn't matter. I didn't know where to look. Her yo-yo was going up and down, almost hypnotizing me, but her white short-shorts were winning the day.

She had a weird look on her face – almost a half-sneer – and I knew that I couldn't read her at all, and that the important thing was that she was standing there. In white short-shorts. And that the others were talking with Decker, and I had wandered off a few feet. I was the one looking at her. It was her and me. Well, me, anyway, looking at her.

These were not Bermuda shorts. These were not gym shorts. There were not anyone's brother's leftover old shorts. These were bright white, tight, very short shorts, that moved with the muscles of her upper thighs and that clung to every shimmy and flex of her astonishing rear.

All I knew about her was that her family moved in four months ago. That was it.

I stared down at my foot and the ground as I casually walked over in her direction, making believe I was kicking something out of my way. I could hear Decker arguing with Gary about whether they were allowed to show tits if a movie was rated "M." ("They *can in a sweater*, or a bra." "Definitely a bikini." "Not by themselves…")

I looked up, and Lynne was watching me approach. She had been the whole time, I imagined. Unfortunately I wasn't quite close enough to say anything to her so I had to close that distance from the middle of the street to the grass strip in front of her sidewalk before anything could be said or heard. The Good Humor ice cream truck turned onto Bay Third Street from St. Mark's Lane and the bells were ringing. She kept doing things with her yo-yo; she wasn't bad and did a trick maneuver of flying it out in front of her, then reeling it back smoothly. She blew a bubble with her gum and it popped.

"Hey," I finally said.

"Hey," she said, whipping her orange toy down and up.

"You came in the middle of the school year, right?" I asked.

"Yup."

"From where?"

"Staten Island."

"Where is that?" I asked.

"It's part of the city. No one thinks of it that way, though."

"So you went to school in the city?"

"It's not like that. 'In the city.' It's near the water. Like this place," she said.

I ran out of things to talk about. We both watched the yo-yo as she commanded it around, and it was clear she'd gotten better at it in the last few minutes. In the background, of course, framing the action was her beautiful legs, those white short-shorts and a striped sleeveless summer shirt.

"How'd you get this good?" I asked, nodding toward her hands.

"Oh, this?" she asked, laughing. "There are instructions when you buy it."

"I never read instructions," I said. "I just start doing things."

"How does that work out?"

"Usually not good," I said, laughing. She smiled, and now it was all worth it. The walking over, crossing the awkward part of the street, the honest report of my own dislike of instructions.

"Is Staten Island Italian?" I asked.

"Well, it's part of the United States," she said. "But pretty much, yeah, it is."

"My cousins are Italian," I said, looking for the connection that would make us paisans.

"But you're not?" she asked.

"No. My mother's sister married a Sicilian."

"I'm only half-Italian," she said. "My mother is Dutch-German."

"Could you teach me yo-yo?" I asked.

I wanted to ask her if she wanted to play house or something. I wanted to play with her, not baseball with the guys. This was the essence of exactly what made guys faggots, according to Decker: wanting to spend time with girls instead of guys. But we were sixteen; weren't we supposed to want to spend time with girls? But doing *what*?

"Yeah, if you get your own," she said.

"Where do you get 'em?" I asked.

"Kay's Stationary. Or Louie's. They both have 'em. You can get ones at Kay's with glitter."

"How come you didn't get one with glitter?"

"I didn't think it was worth an extra dollar. I like when solid colors spin."

"You play any other sports? I asked, immediately knowing it sounded stupid.

"This isn't really a sport," Lynne said.

"I know... I just meant…"

"Yeah. No. I don't really have a sport."

"Ever play tennis?" I asked. "There are great courts down behind the junior high." It was true; when Steve and my friend Glen used to play with me there, we'd do round-robins, in which the loser sat down and let the two others play almost all day long. Someone would ride their bike to 7-11 or Louie's' and pick up sodas and chips and we were good until sundown. But I'd never done it with a girl.

"I'm a spaz," she said, scrunching her face up and dipping a little at the knees. "Really."

"I'm pretty bad, too," I said, not quite honestly. "Maybe I didn't read the directions. You wanna meet there at 10:30 tomorrow morning and try to hit the ball around?"

There wasn't even a pause. "Okay," she said. "But I don't have a racquet."

"I can bring two. And balls."

We both looked away for that one.

"So I'll see you there at 10:30?" I said, half-turning to leave.

"Yeah, okay. Oh, by the way, what's your name?" she asked. "I'm Lynne."

When I got back to the baseball game, they ragged on me for having left the game, making it necessary to substitute a drooling younger kid, Andrew, from down the block for me.

"Where'd you go? A gay nightclub?" Decker asked.

"He was right down the street talking to that girl," Glen volunteered, pointing towards Lynne's house.

"You mean the really ugly one?" Decker asked.

I looked at him and he looked at me, and I wanted to crack his skull. I really wanted to hurt him.

Instead I walked home. Decker continued to say stuff, but as I walked away, I drowned out whatever he was saying by muttering things aloud about him and his sister. "Low-life, redneck trash-collecting, scummy fire-setters…"

When I came in my mother asked where I'd been.

"Playing baseball in the street, why?"

"I wanted to ask you to do something. Tomorrow, Joan, Norma, and I are going to a conference at Dowling College, and Jody has nothing to do."

"So?"

"I'd like you to look after her. You could include her in whatever activities you have planned. She'd love it."

"You're kidding, right?" I asked.

"No, I'm not."

"What about Dad?"

"He's working," she said.

"What about one of her little friends?"

"She can't find one to do anything with tomorrow. I need you to just say 'yes.' What did you have planned anyway? It's just a regular Saturday."

"I don't want to do it," I said, walking sharply in the direction of the stairs towards my room.

"You're going to do it," she said.

"What is this conference about, anyway?"

"It's the National Organization of Women. It's about the Equal Rights Amendment."

"So I have to have my Saturday wrecked because of the National Organization for Women? How is that even fair? I'm not a woman."

"What were you going to do?" She looked at me skeptically. "You're not doing drugs with your friends, are you?"

"No! I was going to play tennis. Tennis, Mom. Is that okay? I was going to ride my bike to school, meet friends, and play tennis."

"Jody would love to do that, too. She has a bike, just pump the tires with air, and make sure she looks both ways before she crosses the street."

The next morning, I couldn't find the air pump for her bike tires. I thought it might be in the trunk of my father's car, and thus at work with him, but my mother told me to borrow a neighbor's so my argument that my sister now couldn't come with me was shot down. Her bike was embarrassing; it was a Barbie model with pink and yellow streamers. It was right for a seven-year-old, and she didn't even seem embarrassed by that. She was dressed for this Saturday adventure in pink shorts and a T-shirt, holding a water bottle, asking me if I could carry it for her in my backpack. Everything she said or did annoyed me.

"What are we doing for lunch?" she asked.

"I don't know. We'll get something."

"You have money?"

"Yes, I have money. You're twelve years old, I'm supposed to pay for you, and I will, okay?"

I was wearing my cool turquoise T-shirt and Bermuda shorts that weren't too loose nor not too tight. I splashed on some English Leather Lime cologne. Jody brought Off bug spray in case there were mosquitos there.

We took off down Bay Third Street, my sister still a little wobbly behind me. I didn't know why it was that Jody was always doing things in a way that looked like she half-expected disaster. She wasn't a confident bicycle rider. She couldn't swoosh and sway the way I could, and I had to deliberately ride slower to look after her, which made me upset even more.

Crossing Main Street – usually a fast maneuver for me; when you saw an opening, you went for it – became something to worry about, because she always hesitated, paused, and wrecked the rhythm. She would start and stop, looking from side to side. It must have been really confusing for cars. By the time we arrived at the back of the school, I tried to ignore feelings of worry. I didn't even know what I was worried about.

I had three racquets on me, sticking out of my backpack. One for me, one for Lynne, and one for Jody. As I unpacked them, I looked around. Lynne wasn't here yet.

"Want to hit some?" my sister asked, as I was peeling back the tab on a fresh can of tennis balls, the vacuum packing giving way, letting the air in with a fast *whoosh*.

"Not yet," I said.

"What am I supposed to do then?" she asked.

"Go look for lost balls. Sometimes people hit them out and they go into those plants all around the other side. And maybe even in the softball outfield back there," I said. "Here's a plastic bag to put the extras in when you find them."

Jody disappeared into the greenery on the far side of the court, and I adjusted my shorts and shirt to look extra casual when Lynne arrived. I spotted her about a quarter-mile away, on an orange bike, coming up the other side of Cottage Street Extension. She weaved across the road, came up the gravel to the courts, stopped, and put down her kickstand.

Lynne had red shorts on today, cut the same way as the white ones, and a striped top that made her shoulders look broad and kind of powerful. I was looking forward to being on the court with her, sending a ball back and forth between us at high velocity. I was sure I could hold my own, even if she hadn't been telling the truth about not being a tennis player. In fact, I wished she were a really good tennis player, so we could really go at it.

"There aren't any!" I heard my sister yell.

I ignored her, but Lynne's head turned in the direction of the shout.

Jody shouted out louder. "Jer? I can't find any. There's not even one over here."

"Are you here with somebody else?" Lynne asked sharply.

"No. I mean, yes. Not really. It's my sister," I said. "She... has to be here today. I mean, I'm supposed to look after her. But she's not really playing with us or anything."

Lynne looked at me with what I thought was the same half-annoyed sneer I'd seen in moments with the yo-yo. "You have to watch her a lot?" she asked.

"No. It's because of the Equal Rights Amendment. My mother went to a meeting today today with the National Organization for Women."

"Oh... she's one of those?" Lynne asked, scrunching up her nose, like something smelled bad.

"Yeah. And she's a school psychologist, too."

"Wow! Okay then..."

"What's your Mom do?" I asked.

"Nothing," Lynne said blankly. "I mean, she does laundry and folds things a lot."

"She a pretty good cook?" I asked, not knowing why.

"No, actually, she isn't. She's pretty bad."

We headed out onto the court.

"So what should I do?" my sister shouted.

"Just come back here," I shouted.

"What?"

"Just come back here!."

I started hitting slow, low lobs towards Lynne, and the first two went into the net. She waited around, racquet down by her long legs, waiting for me to engage her in something fun.

"So what am I supposed to do?" my sister yelled, as she got closer. When she saw Lynne, she stopped and said, "Hi. You know my brother?"

"Not really," Lynne said.

"You live on Bay Third?" Jody asked.

"Yup."

"Do you have any brothers or sisters?"

"I have a sister, but she's older. She lives in Plainview."

"Oh." Jody stood there, waiting for direction.

"Here's what you can do: When we hit the balls into the net, and they don't bounce back to us, you could run and get them, okay? And throw them back to us, either one of us."

"Why can't I play?" she asked.

"Because you can't. Because it's one and one," I said.

"Why can't it be two and one?"

"Because it can't," I said.

"Could I play the winner?"

"I don't know. Maybe," I said. "For now ... just... sit over there on the side. Near the net."

At first she did. Jody scampered up and got the balls each time they got trapped at the net, tossing them back to us. But she got bored quickly. She started bouncing a ball, distracted, then found a wall to throw it against, catching it as it ricocheted off.

Lynne was doing a good job of sending the ball back to me each time. More than once I whiffed, completely missing it, as I realized my eyes were more focused on her body more than the location of the arriving ball. Seeing her body in motion only made me want to see *more* of her body in motion. The hot, shimmering sun, soothing breeze and Lynne's legs taking long, athletic strides had me mesmerized.

"Want to keep score?" I asked after she missed a lob.

"What are we doing for lunch again?" my sister yelled.

"I said I'd take care of it," I shouted, as I slammed a ball back far enough to the right side of the court to force Lynne to run quickly, nearly diving awkwardly to make contact. The more awkward she looked, the more I wanted more of her. She walked to the net slowly once she composed herself.

"Why are you being such a jerk to her?"

I felt stung. "What are you talking about?"

"Your sister. You're being a jerk. She's here, let her play on your side."

"How can you play two against one?"

"You can. It's called Canadian doubles. You use the singles lines for 'out' on my side, the doubles lines on your side for 'out.' And you alternate the person serving."

"How do you know this stuff?" I asked.

"My sister was varsity tennis," Lynne said.

"You said you didn't know how to play," I said.

"I don't really. I never learned. She never did anything with me. I was young. But she left a whole bunch of books and magazines behind when she left. You didn't think I'd show up here letting you know everything and me knowing nothing, right?"

"Hey, Jody," I shouted. "Grab your racquet and come on out. You're going to play on my side."

Lynne paced around on the other side of the net, looking like some sort of long-legged panther, waiting to strike, while I conferred with my sister. "Just ... have fun, okay? Try not to screw up. You stay on this side. If it comes down the middle it's my ball because it's my forehand. Don't try to hit it as a backhand."

"How are you supposed to hold this thing?" my sister asked, slowly rotating the racquet in her hand.

"Here... let go of it. Make believe you are shaking hands with it. And curl your second finger up here a little. And keep it like that, at that angle."

"It feels weird," she said.

"I know it does. It feels weird, and then you get used to it." I demonstrated how to swing, my arm over hers, guiding her. "You have to meet the ball at the sweet spot when it comes to you. When you can do this for a while I'll show you how to hit from low to high when you swing."

"I'll try," my sister said, smiling.

"All right!" I shouted to Lynne. "We're ready. Let's volley to see who serves. Three times over the net, whoever wins the point serves."

The volley was surprisingly long. Lynne kept hitting to me, on my side, either up close to the net or far back, but when it did finally come to Jody, she was able to return it, even though she hit lobs that went thirty feet in the air. Lynne set me up at the net with a super sweet slow shot, and I pounded it. It sped off my racquet and went sailing across the court on an impossible to get diagonal. Lynne ran frantically after it, her red shorts pumping, long arms flailing. The serve was mine.

"You stand in the opposite box, on a diagonal, to receive the serve," I instructed Lynne. "Jody, you are back on this side." Both girls obediently shuffled to their places. "I'd stand a few feet back if I were you." I offered to Lynne. "You want enough room to react in any direction." She made the adjustment. I threw the ball up, reached up to meet it, and powered it directly into the far corner of the box, just in, but unreachable.

"Fifteen-love," I shouted.

"What is 'love' again?" Lynne asked.

"Nothing," I said.

Then I double-faulted. Two serves, both long.

"What does that make it?" Lynne asked.

"Fifteen-fifteen."

"When do I serve?" she asked.

"After the first game is over."

"Do they have bathrooms here?" my sister asked.

I was about to say something when I felt Lynne staring at me, eyes boring into me, waiting for my response to Jody.

"I think the school is open," Lynne volunteered. "I can go with you." And then everyone put down their racquets and walked away.

"Okay. I want to go into school, too," I said, trying to catch up. "I want to see what it looks like in summer."

The hallways were quiet and dark. You had to know where the bathrooms were to find them. I wandered past them, looking at the empty main office. It was strange, like there had been a war and everyone was gone, having retreated to Denmark or something. I could hear the custodians, cleaning and waxing the floors in the wing that included the guidance and attendance offices.

I took a right and walked down into the band room, my favorite room in the school. Here huge tympani drums stood waiting all summer for someone to hit them, two stately old pianos quietly looked on and the conductor stand where in a few months, Mr. Carlino would try to coax some upcoming holiday music out of forty to sixty ninth through twelfth graders was powerfully empty. It was exciting being in there alone. I stood with my back against the wall, taking it all in and remembering last year's winter concert when we played Leroy Anderson's "Sleigh Ride," and it wasn't bad, including the horse-whinnying sound at the end. I started humming it, when the door suddenly opened.

Before I could take in what was happening, Lynne was pressing into me, pushing me hard up against the wall and searching for my mouth with hers. I let my mouth open, even though I was breathless and I felt her lips against mine, her tongue tickling into my mouth. My body instantly reacted; it was amazing how hardwired one's dick and balls were to the excitement of being kissed, but before I could believe my good luck or that this was real, all the lights in the band room went on at once. Jesus Christ, we'd been discovered! But no, it was just that she'd pushed me against all the light switches when she'd made her move, and my back had turned them all on, lighting up the room.

Here was the best part; Lynne didn't even care. She *kept* pressing into me and kissing me with strength. All the strength that I imagined in a cross-court tennis rally from those shoulders was in a full-court pressed up against my body. I suddenly realized how much taller she was than I was. Despite this, her breasts pushed into my chest arching up and forward. Her tongue tickled more deeply into my mouth, into the corners.

After a few amazing seconds, I put both of my hands on her shoulders and pushed her away.

A Foot In the River
(Part 2)

#

I could still feel the after effects of her tongue exploring my mouth, the tingling, but I had, in fact, pushed her away.

"What…was…I mean…" I didn't even know what to say. I wanted her mouth back on mine. I couldn't believe this was happening.

"I know…" she said. "Same. This isn't an every day thing for me, okay?"

"Where's my sister?" I asked. It was the only thing I could think of to say.

"She's meeting us in the art room one-twenty-seven. I said I was getting you."

We walked slowly there, very close to each other, almost shoulder to shoulder. I kept feeling invisible sparks between the molecules of her shoulder and mine. I wasn't sure if I was supposed to hold her hand or not. I was thinking probably yes. I kept thinking about how she'd just said *us*. Meeting "us."

Only my sister wasn't in the art room 127. The janitor, Dominic, saw us snooping around trying to find Jody and yelled at us, "You're not supposed to be in here. Get out unless you have a reason."

"Have you seen my sister?" I asked him.

"Who?"

"My sister. She's twelve, blonde hair."

"No. Now get out."

"Have a nice day," Lynne offered, giving him a little flip of her hand.

I fully expected to see her on the tennis courts, standing where I stood, practicing her serve, which was pretty bad. But she wasn't there. And her bike was gone.

"Well, this ... isn't too good," I said, half out loud, half thinking to myself.

"She do these things a lot?" Lynne asked.

"Never," I said.

"Well ... there's a first time for everything, right?" Lynne said, smiling.

"Where do you think she is?" I asked. "I'm supposed to be looking after her."

"Home," Lynne said factually.

If Jody rode home and succeeded in crossing Main Street without getting flattened, she'd know the way to get into the house. The key was in a well hidden small storage space, disguised as a rock. My parents hadn't given her her own key yet, even though I had one.

"I think I should head home," I said.

"I can come. I don't mind," Lynne said. I found myself feeling good inside even though I was worried about Jody.

We zoomed across Main Street together, crossing at the same time, Lynne to my right, and we raced each other down South Bay Avenue, Lynne putting her legs to excellent advantage and showing that she could beat me there any time of day or night. We weaved left on Bay Third and zoomed toward my driveway, hopping off the bikes before they'd fully stopped moving. I didn't see Jody's bike anywhere in sight. Lynne leaned hers against the maple tree on the right side of the driveway and I put my down on the side. We went to the front door and knocked.

There was no answer, and it sounded silent inside, except

for the scampering sound and barking of our dog, Pepper. I used my key to unlock the door, and we went in. Pepper kept barking at Lynne, but his tail was wagging. He sniffed at her calves intently.

"You have a dog?" I asked.

"Yeah. Petey."

"He smells Petey."

I looked for any sign of Jody, then yelled upstairs, "Jody? Johhhdd? Jody?"

Nothing but silence and the sound of Pepper sniffing, a little higher up Lynne's legs.

"Can I see your room?" Lynne asked.

I pondered this quickly and said, "Sure." We walked to it at the end of the hall, and I opened the door. Lynne walked in and looked around approvingly. Surprisingly to me, there wasn't that much to be embarrassed about in there. The Old Spice deodorant and English Lime aftershave made me feel proud, because it let Lynne know she was in the presence of a *man*.

"It smells good in here," she said. Her hands joined behind her, her nose up in the air.

"Let's go," I said. "Plan B."

"What's Plan B?" she asked.

"I'm making it up; I don't know. Help me think like a twelve-year-old girl," I asked.

"A friend's house?" Lynne guessed.

"The only friend I know she has, Wendy Kinsley, lives in Brightwaters."

"Couldn't we call?" she reasoned.

"I don't know her number or exact address," I said. "I just know what the house looks like, because we drop her off there sometimes."

"Is she her *best*, best friend?" Lynne asked.

"Yes."

"Then let's take a ride. I can come with you, if I stop off at home first and leave a note. I have to tell them when I'll be home. Brightwaters is at least four miles away. My house is on the way ... it's..."

"I know where it is," I said, cutting her off. "I pass it every day."

Lynne looked at me, and her face opened into the nicest smile.

I gave Pepper a Milk-Bone and we locked up, zooming out on our bikes, leaning them on the telephone pole in front of Lynne's house.

"No one's home," she said, unlocking the door with a key on a long green lanyard she pulled from her pocket. "Wanna come in?"

I nodded, and we walked to her kitchen. I stood near her and looked over her left shoulder as she wrote, "Went for a long bike ride with a friend, home later. Tennis was fun. Don't worry!" Then she drew a heart and wrote "Lynne" underneath. She quickly put down the pen, whirled and grabbed me, pushing up against me like before, kissing again.

I didn't protest. I was about to say, "I'm worried about my sister," when Lynne asked, eyes flashing, "Wanna see my room?" She led by the hand and I supposed it was fair enough because she'd seen mine.

Her room had decorations on the door, swirly things in purple and pink, and when she opened the door I saw a poster of *The Mod Squad* on her wall. Pete, Linc, and Julie looking so damn cool and beyond these things, beyond Bay Third Street, looking so Californian and powerful and undercover, which they were, ready to play by nobody's rules, ready to groove to new music. Lynne actually looked like Peggy Lipton a bunch, especially on the poster, in which Julie was looking up with big eyes, her nose turned slightly up, her lips serious, but still approachable. She was looking like she could somehow see the future or at least was one step ahead of everyone else. Lynne's room smelled like citrus, and I looked to the side of her bed, where I saw two bottles: Love's Fresh Lemon Cleanser and its companion, Love's Fresh Lemon Cologne.

That's when she tackled me, laughing. We landed on her bed and she was on top, rolling, and kissing, our bodies working on a separate, more serious, rhythm of connection than our laughter admitted. I really liked having her on me like this, and she seemed to be into this at least as much as me, maybe more.

For a half second I wanted to have last for all time, I didn't worry about where my sister was or what would happen if she got home without me, telling my mother everything, or didn't get home safely at all. I wanted every inch of Lynne to continue playing with and touching every inch of me. And every inch of me was deliciously expanding in the moment.

"We've got to..."

"I know. We have to find your sister," she said, giving a final wriggle of her upper torso against me, nailing me with a tongue kiss again. "I'm just about ready... to go," she said, pushing off of me and rolling aside.

There was no way now that my erection was NOT showing, outlined hard against my shorts. I prayed she didn't notice. Instead as she got up, she put her hands over her mouth, eyebrows raised, and with slow, shocked-sounding pleasure said, "Oh *my* God!," looking right at it.

I murmured something; she asked, "Should I... should we...?"

"No. We've got to go. It's all okay," I lied in complete confusion. This felt the most naked I'd ever been in front of a girl, even though we both were completely clothed. I had the incredible knowledge and sensation that it could go a lot further in one second's notice. I felt a surge of hunger for her and walked over to her, pressing myself up against her, letting her feel all of me as I reached around and felt the muscular globes or her butt. We both sank into the embrace and kissed some more. Her mouth was more open than before, and she seemed slower and almost hypnotized as we kissed. Or I was hypnotized, or we both were by the very hotness of what we were feeling. We broke the embrace.

We left the room, locked up, and hopped on our bikes. I was riding on a cloud, and I couldn't get the Stones' song, "Get Off Of My Cloud" out of my head. Maybe we were both on a cloud, maybe the same one.

"Where are we going?" she asked.

"Not sure," I said, and I wasn't. "A cloud."

"What?"

"I guess Brightwaters."

We took shortcuts to Montauk Highway, but there was still Main Street in Bay Shore to get through. It was a busy place. Some of it we rode in the street, but there was so much crazy parking going on that we took to the smooth Bay Shore sidewalks instead. We weaved around the corny-looking pedestrians, with a few of them scowling because kids as big as we were weren't supposed to be riding on the sidewalks anymore. Next year all the kids I knew, plus me, would be working summer jobs. This was still a summer for cruising around and laughing.

I tried imagining my sister making this very scary ride by herself, and I wondered if she took to the sidewalks, too, and if people would've been kinder to the Barbie-bike riding wobbly rider/kid that she was. I wondered if I should yell at her when I found her.

"Can we get a Slurpee on the way back?" Lynne shouted.

"I don't see why not," I shouted back to her, trying to sound nice, but ending up sounding like a dad. This happened a lot lately; I would try to sound nice or smart and it would sound too adult. I guess I was thinking more like an adult sometimes, but feeling more like a kid usually and sometimes my serious side would betray me.

"You don't know the address?" Lynne shouted.

"No ... just the way there," I said. I wondered what it meant that this was starting to be a big pattern for me: knowing how to get places and not knowing any road names at all. I wondered if that meant I'd fail my road test when it came time to drive. We'd taken turns taking the lead on the sidewalks into Brightwaters, but I passed her to guide us onto a left turn onto South Windsor Avenue.

"You know what?" she shouted. I looked back at Lynne, her hair flying behind her in the wind. She really *did* look like Peggy Lipton. I started to wish I could be in the *Mod Squad* with her, but then realized that in a way, I already was. I could imagine Linc falling into our phalanx of bicycle-riding undercover agents at the next cross street, Windsor Place, with background music. "I'm having fun," she shouted. "Are you?"

"Yes, I am. But we have to find my sister. No kidding. Then it'll be more fun," I said.

"You know she's fine, right?" Lynne shouted.

"I don't know that."

We pulled up at Wendy Kinsley's house, and we walked up to the door. We rang the doorbell and then knocked at the door. Nothing happened, and there was no movement in the house. There wasn't even a dog. We walked behind the shrubs to look into the window of the living room; a cat rubbed up against the window from the other side, looking back at us with a questioning look.

"Let's look around back," I said.

We did. It was all locked tight and silent.

We walked around front again and sat down on the front lawn to strategize. That's when the Suffolk County Police car rolled up, parking slowly in front of the grass. As it did, the cop turned on the blue light and the siren made one fast *whoop*. Then he turned the car off and walked over toward us. The light kept flashing on the top of the car even though the car was off.

"You two have some form of ID on you?" he asked.

"No, sir," I said.

"No," Lynne said.

"What are you doing here? You don't live on this block, do you?" he asked.

"No," we said in unplanned unison.

"Then why are you here?"

"Looking for my sister and her friend," I said, briskly.

"Who is her friend?" the cop asked, seeming to hope I'd trip up.

"Wendy Kinsley."

"How do you know the Kinsleys?" he asked.

"I don't really. My sister does. She's twelve-years-old and I don't know where she is. I was watching her, but we got sidetracked in the junior high school, and she's not at home, and we'd thought she'd be here."

"School's out for the summer. Why are we talking about school?" he asked, eyes narrowing.

Lynne stepped forward and said, "We were playing tennis at Islip Junior High, and we were watching his sister for the day. We went to go to the bathroom, and his sister said she'd meet us in the art room, only she wasn't there. When we looked for her, her bike was gone."

He looked at me again suspiciously, as if he suspected

there was a missing part to the story. There was – the band room kiss.

"You're not doing a very good job of looking out for her then, are you?" he asked.

I didn't say anything.

"*Are you?*" he asked again.

"I guess not," I offered.

"And if you knew anything about the Kinsleys, you'd know they are on vacation this week and away. We have an 'away' list, and while we can't check up on everybody, we do our best to keep our eyes open for suspicious activity. You qualify. Were you peeking in the windows, walking behind the shrubs?"

"Yes," I said.

"Why were you doing that – if you weren't planning to break in? Why do you think they have shrubs there in the first place? They call it a front door for a reason now, don't they?"

We were both quiet now.

"Are you kids on drugs?"

"No, sir," we said in unison.

"Do you see how a reasonable person could think you were planning to break in?" he asked.

"Yes," Lynne said quickly.

"I guess," I said.

"Well, your guess would be right. I understand that you are upset about your sister, so I'm going to cut you some slack. We can help find her if you give us some information. When did you last see her?"

He took out his pad and started writing down what we were saying, after getting our names. What we said was pretty accurate, leaving out only the lost time spent making out in Lynne's house.

"We're going to send a cruiser to your house first. Little

girls on Barbie bikes tend to ride home," he said.

"Good idea," I said, trying to not sound sarcastic. "But I think no one is home."

"We're going to try it first. If that doesn't pan out, how can we contact your parents?" he asked. I didn't want to give out my father's pharmacy work number, so I told him about my mother being down at the college for the day for the Equal Rights Amendment workshop.

He snorted. "Wow… okay … little girl running around, unsupervised, mom at women's lib meeting … whatever floats your boat, right? What time does that meeting get done?"

"I don't know. They talk a lot. It usually goes an hour past when they say it'll end," I said. This was true. "They just keep talking."

Lynne asked him gently, in a mixture of a little-girl voice and a teenaged one, "Can we ride our bikes back to the tennis courts to double-check? We really weren't breaking in."

He looked at Lynne, if I weren't mistaken, slowly, up and down, and then said, "Why not?" We'll tell the cruiser to swing by there after your house. Hey: Next time, call the police first. That's what we're here for."

"Thank you, Officer," I said.

"Thank you," Lynne said, smiling and waving good-bye with three fingers of her right hand.

We kept to the streets of Bay Shore on the ride back. I was hoping hard that my mother hadn't left the ERA workshop early for any reason because if Jody was home, she'd be home alone. I didn't know if there was some law about how old you had to be to be left alone, and I hoped for a simple ending to this day.

We came up on the tennis courts and there was my sister, sitting on the ground crying, curled over, a big paper bag in front of her. Her shoulders were heaving up and down, and she sobbed into her hands. I felt terrible, as if all the worry I'd ever had about her – since the day she was born, when I took a vow to protect my beautiful baby sister through her entire life, whatever it took – had been true and necessary.

"What happened?" I asked, kneeling by her side and putting an arm around her.

"I went to get lunch for all of us," she said, between sobs.

"How did…?"

"I went home to get money. I have some money of my own. I used the key. And I rode to Louie's Luncheonette, and came back here after getting stuff. And no one was here." She let loose, really crying now. "I wanted to surprise you."

Lynne kneeled down on the other side of her, too, flashing a look that seemed to say, *I told you she was okay*. She put her hand on the back of my sister's head and stroked her hair some as she asked, in a soothing voice, "What things did you get?"

Jody choked out the words, in between drawing back up the mucous that was coming from her nose as she cried, saying, "Sandwiches. And potato chips. And peanut butter cups for you, Jerry. And 7-Ups."

I was without words. Peanut butter cups and 7-Up were my favorite things.

"That had to cost a lot of money," Lynne said. "That was really generous. Is it okay if I chip in some toward it? My share? I'm sure your brother wants to, too."

"Okay," my sister said.

"Here is $3.00, for mine," said Lynne, taking money out of the pockets of her tight shorts. Lynne then looked at me.

"I have the money for both you and me; it's from Mom," I said, sounding again caught in between being myself and being an adult. "How much was the total?"

Jody looked at me and seemed to want to hit me. "I don't

need your money," she said. "Just pay for yourself. Give $3.00, like Lynne did."

"But I had more stuff. The peanut butter cups."

"Fine, give $3.50."

I dug it out of my pocket and gave it to her. She took it and we sat in silence.

"What was it like crossing Main Street?" I asked finally.

"Easier the second time," Jody said. "I'm here, right?"

Just as she said that, a police car drove up. Once again, flashing lights on the top as it pulled over, but no siren *whoop* this time.

The policeman, a different guy, because this was a different car, asked, "Is this your sister? You are Jerry S. and Lynne D.?"

"Yes. And this is my sister, Jody," I said.

"Happy ending, then?" he asked.

"Very," I said.

"Have a nice day," he said, pulling away.

We sat and ate everything Jody bought. The peanut butter cups were perfect, and I shared them with Lynne and my sister, both of whom resisted at first. The sun was starting to get low in the sky, but there was enough time for three more Canadian doubles games before we headed off to Bay Third Street together.

Lynne peeled off to go home first. "Next time we get the Slurpees," I shouted to her. She smiled and leaned into her right-hand turn, already in progress. I waved good-bye, and she waved back. Jody and I went home. We walked in, and it was empty and dark. We turned on the lights, let Pepper out back, then fed him. It felt familiar and cozy. We closed the wooden blind slats up in the TV room, something we did every night. Maybe my mother would bring home something for dinner.

"What would you have said if the police brought you back home, and mom was here? She would've been scared to death," I asked Jody.

She thought about it for a minute, then said, "I would've told her that I took care of lunch myself. Like an Equal Rights thing."

That made sense to me. We turned on the outside porch light and settled into the TV room, forgetting whose night it was to choose.

Outside, the mosquito-control truck, which patrolled our little village by the bay on a monthly basis, sprayed its fog of chemical mist over the lawns and backyards of our home. The mist rose under the street lamps to create the strangest of fogs. Stranger still was how it smelled

I thought of Lynne, safely in *her* house, both of us insulated from the chemical mist. And how we'd see each other in the light of day, me knowing that my days playing baseball in the street with the guys was suddenly over.

Above-Ground Pool

#

The tangy, sharp ultra-vinegar smack in the face smell of formaldehyde filled the room, replacing my personal cloud of Jade East aftershave. I'd worn the Jade East every day of school since eighth grade. Once I started making my own sandwiches, I could taste it on the peanut butter and jelly sandwiches five hours later, because I always made sandwiches after slapping Jade East onto my face. I guess it didn't wash off easily.

Mr. Steadman stood in front of the tall lab counter in the front of the room, black plastic trays with dead frogs in front of him. Each one was laid on its back, hands up next to the head in green, dead total surrender.

"Each of you will get a knife. You are *responsible* for this knife; it is *your* knife for forty-seven minutes. It will be turned in at the end of the period. Failure to hand it back in when I collect them *will* result in a failing grade for the semester, a trip to Mr. Tuffin's office, *and* a call home. Without exception."

Handing a sharp X-acto knife to laughing ninth graders didn't strike me as a good idea in the best of times, and these weren't the best of times. Nine months in high school hadn't proven more fun than junior high. Teacher warnings about not being able to get away with last year's immature behaviors – "forgetting" homework, arriving late to class, or flicking a classmate on their ear quickly when no one was looking – were turning out to be true. We spent most of the year trying to invent *new* immature behaviors.

I wished the high school yearbook photographer had been there to get a picture of Mr. Steadman in front of the corpses in trays, hands on hips, his concerned "Don't try to get over on me" look trying without success to convince us that he was some sort of tough guy. He always wore short-sleeved dress shirts that looked like his mother had picked them out for him and bought them ten at a time in slightly different colors, all of them a variation on neutral. Not only was Mr. Steadman *not* a tough guy, he was notoriously, the opposite: The guy who'd drank a beaker of chemical poisons in front of last year's chemistry class the day after Valentine's Day, had done months in a mental hospital, and come back to be reassigned to the ninth grade (dead frogs replacing chemical temptations). Kids said that he in fact still live at home with his parents, had no wife, and no one knew of him ever having had a girlfriend.

"Come up to get your specimen. Single file, please."

I waited in line behind Kitty Colucci. I could usually smell either her Herbal Essence hair shampoo or some body spray from a few feet away, but now all I could smell was well-preserved amphibian flesh. I stared at the frog..I didn't want to be here, knife in hand, any more than it wanted to be dead on its back in a tray.

"Those of you who requested fetal pigs, please step out of line, form a separate single-file line, and come get your specimen," Mr. Steadman announced.

I was sticking with the frog; Perry Hendow went with the pig. It was a mere thirty-seven minutes now before lunch period, and Perry did his best imitation of a grown-up chef at a fancy restaurant: "We have a few specials today: dead frog in saline with a formaldehyde sauce, or fetal pig with cream sauce and mushrooms." He then balanced his tray like a dainty French waiter and danced away from Mr. Steadman's desk toward his own.

Behind him, Laura Decker turned, put her hand over her stomach, and puked, two floods of vomit pulsing from her mouth, splattering onto the floor. The room immediately took on a mixed formaldehyde and teenage puke tangy scent. Kids immediately and loudly shouted, "Ewwwww!"

Steadman directed Sandra Meadows to get a bucket right away and Kitty Colucci to "Take her out, take her to the nurse! Perry! Stop fooling around. Get the janitor now." Perry gave a little bow like any proper French waiter or maitre d' would, setting his fetal pig down on the desk and disappearing into the hallway, and kids quickly moved their desks away from the pool of puke on the floor.

"We are not done. Go back to work. You are *responsible for this assignment*," Steadman bleated.

"May I be excused to go to guidance?" Kevin Wheeler asked in his ultra-smart kid voice, as if he were better than the rest of us and didn't have to sit through this, let alone cut the midsection of a frog or pig open to see what the insides looked like.

I held the knife in my hand, but didn't want to use it. Debby Drucker popped her hand up and asked Steadman the same thing, and I was wondering, *Can you just watch someone else do it? The dissection?*

How come it was girls who always said what I was thinking, not guys? Why did I think like a girl? What was my problem?

I stared back at my frog; it looked very peaceful.

"Cut from about one-half inch down from the mouth the length of it, to open the abdomen," Steadman said.

There was a sudden movement of chairs in the far left corner of the room and two kids were standing up around Julie Barker, who was crying. She had her glasses off, on the desk, and was trying to gulp back tears, but we'd already heard them.

"It's dead, dummy," Ricky Rapisardi shouted.

That seemed to make Julie release the breath that she'd been holding and burst out into tears louder than before. "Get her a tissue," Mr. Steadman shouted as Ricky and Sal Moffet laughed louder than before.

"The dead frog is coming to life, Julie! It's coming to get you!" one of them shouted.

Steadman leaned on his teacher's desk and sputtered his usual, "People! People!" warning.

I turned to David, my smart best friend since fifth grade, and nodded toward the frog. "Are you going to cut it?"

"I think it's required," he said.

"Why can't they just do one and have us all look?" I asked.

"Maybe each one is different," David theorized.

"That can't be, David, c'mon. They're all frogs. In the same frog family. They have to have the same guts."

"Well ... think about you and your sister Jody. Pretty different, right?"

"Yeah, but our guts are probably similar."

"Do your own work," Steadman shouted. "There will be no way to evaluate you if you don't do your own work, and this *will be reflected in your final grade* as it will count as an 'Incomplete.'"

Perry was back in the room now with no janitor in sight, and he went right back to his fetal pig, carrying it like it was a Thanksgiving turkey, then balancing it on his fingertips, while singing circus music: "Da-da-DA-TA-da-dada-da-DA!" before Steadman caught him.

"In your own seats! At your own table!"

"Which is it?" Perry shouted. "Our seat or a table?"

"That's it! Perry! Tuffin! Now!"

Terry did his completely innocent face, turned his head on an angle, and looked at Steadman in shock, before turning to the rest of us, his jury of his own peers. "What did I do?" he asked. "I wasn't even laughing."

"Tuffin! *Now*! Put down your pig."

"Will it be here for me tomorrow?" he asked.

"No. And return the knife. What we did today is the assignment. You didn't complete yours so ... there's your incomplete. *In the book.*"

"That's no fair. You stopped me from doing it. Then you told me I didn't do it. That's not exactly a *stable* thing to do," Perry said, venturing into the unspoken mental-health territory that was always just beneath the surface in Steadman's class.

"What did you say?" Steadman asked, his eyes narrowing. "What did you just say?"

"I said that wasn't fair," Perry said.

"That's not what you said."

"It was," Perry insisted.

Steadman started blinking too many times in a row. I thought he might pass out or go into some kind of convulsion.

"Get out!" he shouted at Perry.

"I just got back from getting the janitor!"

"Out!"

Perry left. I held the tip of the X-acto knife to the throat of the frog. I couldn't do it. I raised my hand.

"What? Yes, Mr. Sander?"

"What if you have religious grounds?" I asked.

"I don't understand the question."

"I'm not supposed to. Religion," I mumbled.

"What religion are you?" he asked, eyes narrowing.

"Jewish."

"So am I. You're allowed to do it."

Steadman was Jewish?

"How do you think people get into medical school without doing this?" he asked. "It's not like you're supposed to eat it!"

"Are you saying I'm supposed to go to medical school just because I'm Jewish?" I asked.

"I'm not going to answer that. That's not a real question. Get to work, Mr. Sander."

"I need to go to the nurse."

"She's not a religious resource."

"I'm going to puke," I said, improvising to get out of there, forcing myself to stare at the slightly dried puddle of puke on the floor and putting my hand over my stomach. I was completely faking it.

"You will lose credit for this assignment."

"I'm going to puke *now*, I think."

"All right, get out. Don't come back today. I don't understand this problem. *People, this* is *essential*. We've been working toward this all year."

The hallway was quiet. I took the long slow walk to the nurse's office. Mrs. Tangelopoulos was famous for being a bad nurse. Some people said that she wasn't one at all, but was like some sort of substitute teacher. All I knew was that she'd told me earlier in the year that I was legally deaf in New York State. I wasn't. She'd also told Barbara Kelly that she was likely pregnant. She wasn't. The important thing, though, was that she'd take your temperature and if it was more than 100 degrees, you'd get to go home. Mine was 98.6 degrees. I told her I was going to throw up anyway, and she had me lay down.

"Do you have any lollipops?" I asked her. (Sometimes she did.)

"No. Just rest."

I hadn't even noticed that Marie Pappas was lying down on the next bed over. They were supposed to pull a curtain between kids to prevent them from spreading kid diseases, but they usually didn't.

"Hi," Marie said, her big brown almond-shaped eyes taking me in.

"Hey," I said. I knew Marie because she was a really good piano player in school, but didn't take lessons from Mrs. Ketcham. I was intrigued by people who had learned how to play but not from Mrs. Ketcham. Aside from wondering how this was even possible, I wondered if they'd learned a whole different way that made them superior to me.

"Want one?" Marie asked, handing me a lollipop.

"How'd you get 'em?" I asked.

"I took the last two," she said, smiling.

I rested my head back on the pillow Mrs. P. had supplied and stretched out, after unwrapping the lollipop and putting it in my mouth. It was cherry. All was good in this moment.

"What are you here for? Are you really sick?" I asked Marie, out of the side of my mouth.

"No," she said. "I had math. Mrs. Leotardi. I told the teacher it was female stuff."

I stole a quick look at Marie, who was smiling. She had what seemed like a year-round tan going.

"How do you stay so tan all year long?" I asked her, turning my head in her direction.

"I'm Italian," she said. "The family's from Sicily."

"Isn't your name Greek?"

"I thought so, too. Someone must've moved," she said, flipping over to look at me directly. "What's your family? Where're they from?"

"Austria. But ... Jewish Austria."

"I didn't know there was one."

"Well, there wasn't really. It's hard to explain. I don't think it was really Austria. No one in the family talks about it. The passports say Austrian-Hungarian Empire. But I think it was ... the Polish part?"

"The Polish part of Jewish Austria? In a larger empire?" she repeated back to me, smiling, her eyes dancing. "Three or four places? Maybe you're the one who is Greek."

"I think it was a very small town, and they got beat up a lot by whoever owned it at the time," I said, flipping onto my side, too.

"No talking, please!" Mrs. T. shouted. "You're here because you're sick! People are trying to get better."

Marie and I looked around; we were the only ones there. We faced each other and whispered.

"But they never owned it?"

"What?"

"The Polish-Austrian town?"

"No. I don't think they even wanted to. What about Sicily?"

"My relatives definitely didn't own it. They just wanted to get out alive."

"Do you ever think about who owns *this* place?"

"Which place? The high school?"

"No, Islip," she said.

"I can't tell. I used to think it was the German or Irish kids. Then it seems like people who *aren't* Irish or Italian or Jewish. Whoever's left. South of Montauk Highway people. WASPs, or something."

"Don't *you* live South of Montauk?" she asked quickly.

"Well... yes." I hadn't thought of that when I was trying to sound smart.

"So does my family. So there goes that theory."

We stared at each other, neither of us really sick.

"Mark Klein is having a pool party this Saturday night, you know. You don't have to be invited. He said just come."

"He is?" I asked. I never knew Mark had a pool. "He has a pool?"

"An above-ground pool. But … it's still a pool party," she said.

I couldn't believe Mark had told her about it and not me. He and I were supposed to be friends. Then I looked at Marie again, at her long, lovely frame, her beautiful tan, and her incredible smile and I thought to myself, *Yeah, Mark, you dog. No wonder I hadn't heard about it.* I wondered what color two-piece bathing suit Marie would look outstanding in. I settled on dark purple.

"I think we're allowed to bring someone if you want," Marie said. "So… I don't know if you're busy, but … maybe I'll see you there?"

My head was spinning, but this was interrupted by the sharp nasal sound of Mrs. T's voice.

"Marie, are you ready to go back now?" Mrs. T. asked, standing about two feet from our cots. We hadn't heard her sneak up on us. "Feeling better?" she asked, looking snarly and not anything like a concerned nurse.

"Yeah, okay I am," Marie said, sitting up and casting me a flashing conspiratorial smile before smoothing out her blouse and jeans and walking off, trying to look half-sick still, looking back at me one more time, as she gathered her hair to the side ruffled it somehow and distributed it back to where it came from, looking better than ever. She wiggled her hands in a little wave to me.

I got sent back to my next class when the bell rang and all I could think about was my two problems for Saturday: *One, what to wear? And two, Kendra.*

Kendra and I were going on year two-and-a-half of some sort of relationship that in an earlier time, we would've called friendship. But we weren't little kids anymore. Kendra was the perfect combination of beautiful, smart, sweet, and careful, which made her someone I truly couldn't figure out. Did she really like me? And would she be willing to *do anything* with me? (That's how it went, right?) Or ... didn't she like me (in which case, should we move on and settle down with a different ninth grader to make out with)?

The two of us never seemed to answer that; we just kept circling around it, telling each other about our days, our families, what made us laugh at school, and what upset us. We did this almost every day. That's why everyone thought we were boyfriend and girlfriend. Half the time we thought that, too. But then we would do some lightweight making out, and she would pull away from it and make me listen to the new Joni Mitchell album. I told her it definitely wasn't Steppenwolf, whom I preferred. We'd go along like not much happened, and I would go home thinking about how really good the making out had been, and we'd check in with each other the next day at school or after, with another make-out session happening two weeks later.

I had no idea whether Kendra knew about Mark's pool party or not. I wouldn't put it past him to have told her and not me about it, just so he could end up with about five girls in his pool with him with maybe no other guys. I was looking forward to seeing his face when I arrived, carrying a few bags of chips and soda, all ready for the party.

But I needed to figure out what to wear. There were two components to this: the what to show up wearing part and which bathing suit to bring. Things that would make me look fat were out. My mother had already let me know for years that shopping in the husky section of boys' clothing stores was the key to success, having once patted me on the butt in Gimbel's in front of my David's mother, saying, "He's a little bit big back *here,* so ... we're going to shop 'husky,'" and even though I'd started to get taller it felt like a nervous line in between where I was and becoming a chubby blob. Fortunately, Mark was challenged in the same way.

I had a Hawaiian shirt in my closet that'd been waiting for an occasion like this. I think it was from the previous year and was nervous about whether it would still fit. The Hawaiian look would go with my nonchalant "Hey, I heard everyone was gathering for a pool party and I thought I'd just stop by" attitude, which I was working on. The question of long pants or shorts was made easier by the realization that the last shorts my mother had bought me were for Camp Encore last year (one in beige and one in grey) and looked really stupid outside of a musical summer-camp environment. They had a ridiculously large number of pockets and the whole thing got puffy in all the wrong places, particularly when my shirt was tucked in. It was decided: It'd be jeans with my Hawaiian shirt worn on the outside, *not* tucked in.

Marie would think it was cool. Or at least not notice it as *uncool.*

I didn't let myself think about what if both Marie and Kendra showed up at the same time.

My mother always shopped on Thursdays, and I made sure to ask her to buy a large bag of Cheetos, a large bag of Ruffles potato chips, and a can of Hawaiian Punch for the party. I told her I had a party to go to, and she seemed pleased that I'd been invited to go to Mark's party. Which wasn't exactly true, but wasn't exactly not true.

"I'm glad you're expanding your social circle," she said. Ever since she started taking classes at Dowling College to get her degree to become a psychologist, she used the biggest words she could. If there was a simple way of saying something, she never took it anymore. ("I didn't think you'd negotiate that turn," she'd say when she was helping me learn how to drive, a second before wrestling the steering wheel from me in life-saving mode. "I don't want any acrimony," she would tell me before a long family car trip. Even my father wasn't sure what she meant. She would change whatever I said into some sort of social commentary, drawing links, it seemed now, between me and the *men* who ran the country and world and who dedicated their waking hours to keeping women "marginalized, controlled, and limited.") It pissed me off.

"I'm not 'expanding my circle,' " I said. "I'm going to Mark's. I already know Mark."

"But there will be others there."

"Yes, everyone I see every day at school, Mom. It's not a big thing. It's just a party. It doesn't change my life. Could you take me there at 8:00? And could I stay til midnight?"

"I want you home by 10:30," she said.

"Nobody is home by 10:30! That's when things get good."

"What is that supposed to mean?" she asked, eyes narrowing. "Does Mark take drugs? Is this a drug party?" She looked the part of the concerned suburban mom in an after-school TV special about drug abuse.

I choked back a laugh. "No one I know has 'drug parties.' Gary probably won't go, because he'll be studying for the SATs or something. Cool people don't even arrive to parties til way later than 8. Could you take me over there at 8:30 instead, and pick me up at midnight?"

"Absolutely not. I will take you over there at 7:30 and will retrieve you at 10:30."

"No one will *even be* there at 7:30! Do *you want* me to get made fun of? Do you want to come into the party and take me by the hand and lead me out just when the party is getting good?"

"You're being reactive," she said.

"I'm *what*?"

"Being reactive."

"*I'm disagreeing* with you," I said.

She suddenly looked very angry. Her eyes flashed, her hair seemed darker and more dangerous than before, pulled back in no-nonsense sharpness. "This is non-negotiable. Do you think because you are a male you have dominion over these decisions? Did you learn that from your father? Your uncle? You are going at 7:30, and I'll pick you up at *eleven*, okay? This is a concession on my part. There won't be any more of them until I'm met by you halfway. That means cleaning up around this house, doing your own laundry, and learning to think of others. Do I make myself clear?"

She had been talking this way for about three months now, ever since she started going to meetings of the National Organization for Women in Bay Shore. She'd ask questions all the time that didn't require an answer. I missed my old mother, the one who was like other kids' mothers.

"Yes, you do," I said. "Thank you for getting the stuff. And ... for the ride." I was learning how to manage her. She walked away the way a boxer returns to their corner when the bell rings in between rounds.

On Friday, no one was talking about the party at Mark's. This seemed odd to me, but I figured that it was one of those things where everyone was keeping it to themselves that they'd been invited and didn't want to mention it to anyone else, in case they hadn't been invited. I hung out with Kendra in between classes and at lunch the usual way we did and talked about Earth Day and how we'd gotten to walk around outside trying to notice natural things around us, but that three kids had cut out, running off into the woods laughing, and that the teachers said that a few bad apples ruined it for the rest of us, which someone made everyone laugh because them saying that that way made it sound like we were living in the 1920s or something. Then lunch was over and I barely saw Kendra in between eighth and ninth period and the day was over. So we never got to talk about the party.

My mother thought it'd be nice for me to bring some sort of health-food mix ("Something that's not junk… ") to the party, too, so at 7:20 p.m. that Saturday I gathered up my Cheetos, Ruffles, and trail mix ("Mountain Roads Blend") and headed off to Mark's, riding shotgun in her white Buick.

"It'd be nice if your father would offer to drive you every now and then," she said, turning up the radio at the same time. The Creedence Clearwater Revival song, "Fortunate Son" came on. I must have snorted. "What? You think it's funny that I'm supposed to be your chauffeur while your father is off playing poker? *Every* week?"

I looked out the window, saw two squirrels chasing each other up a telephone pole, then closed my eyes and zoned out. The air conditioning was off – what was the point of having air conditioning if you never used it? – and the car was bouncing up and down on its soft suspension with the heat of the day lulling me to near sleep. I closed my eyes and imagined the party.

Marie was there and the dark blue two-piece she was wearing looked so casual and perfect, she could've been a model or a movie actress, walking around in it like it was no big deal, even though other people were still in their party clothes. Her olive skin tone made her look exotic at the same time as just what she was: the girl practically next door. The girl from another piano teacher. Forbidden fruit. What if

Kendra walked in?

Then someone suggested that before we hit the swimming pool we form a circle and play Spin The Bottle with an newly emptied Boone's Farm Apple wine bottle, one of several that kids were drinking and passing around without cups. There was a lot of laughter and the next thing I knew, Sandra Meadows was spinning, and she got me and came over and sat in my lap and gave me an incredibly long, wet kiss on the mouth. It was great. Sandra was famous for having disrupted Mrs. Berkowitz's English class by entering three minutes late with Kitty Colucci, both of them wearing skirts way too short for school. She had gotten sent to the office and they called home. Her mother, they said, laughed it off and she wore the same skirt the next day.

Our kiss had lasted longer than I ever had hoped and kids were going *"Whoa!,"* before she broke it off, hopped off me, and returned to her seat in the circle across from me. I wondered if Marie was jealous and shot her a quick look. I couldn't tell. She had one of those neutral girl faces that could mean anything.

Then Anne Littit spun and ... also got me! Anne lived only one block over from me, but we never hung out, even though I admired her blonde hair and smile every time I rode past on my bike, and she was outside helping her mother with the plants. She jetted across the circle over to me fast as kids started *oohing* and *ahhing* about my luck. "Whoah, *Jerry*! Y'know if you get three, it's Seven Minutes in Heaven with anyone you choose!" I hadn't known that. Kathy's kiss was crisp but firm. She hopped back to her place in the circle as Greg Lefliger grabbed the bottle to spin. *Don't get Marie*, I thought and prayed. *Don't get Marie.*

He got Trish Walker, the red-headed new transfer student girl from West Islip. He looked like a wolf as he approached her, and he started making wolf sounds. Everyone laughed. He sat next to her and they kissed, with him shifting the angle of his mouth several times.

Marie was next. She still was the only girl wearing a two-piece at the moment. I tried to look nonchalant as she grabbed the bottle and gave it an extra vigorous spin.

It got me. She got me. The crowd noise rose quickly, "Seven Minutes in Heaven! Seven Minutes in Heaven!"

"Where?" she asked, blushing.

"In that back room!" someone shouted. She came over, walking slowly, one hand trying to shield her face, embarrassed, turning red (well, olive-red) while the other hand reached for me, pulling me up to my feet. I walked off with her to the back room as the circle whooped and whistled. I could hear *"All right!"* and *"Sander!,"* along with a few "You go, Marie! Go get him!"

Then Kendra walked in and saw us.

The car hit a bump and I shot up, awake. I was in the front seat, with my mother. "You haven't heard a thing I said ..." she said, sharply, snapping me out of my horny teenage reverie. I woke up, still in the Buick. "Were you dreaming? I asked you the same question three times. Do you have some sort of minimal brain dysfunction? Or is that only when I'm driving you and asking you questions you'd rather ignore?"

"We're here," I said, pointing to the modest little development house across the street. "Thank you for the drive. And the trail mix," I said, hopping out, holding the bags of my party contributions in my hands. "I'll be sure to share it."

"12 o'clock," she said sharply. "Not 12:01. Not 12:05."

I ruffled my hair in the right places, slamming the car door shut. It was a little lighter than a major door slam statement would've been. "Mom, one thing: Minimal brain dysfunction? They don't call it that anymore. They call it ADHD now. The books you read may be old. I'll promise I'll see you at midnight. Thank you again."

I bolted before I could see her full reaction, but she looked like she was gathering her full force for a counterattack.

I walked up to Mark's front door and knocked. The door opened almost immediately, and I looked down to see Mark's round little sister poking her glasses up into place. She had to be nine or ten. "Hi ... it's one of Mark's friends, Mom!" she called.

"Is Mark there? Am I allowed in?"

"Hold on. Wait a minute." She closed the door three-quarters of the way and I heard feet scuffling around. "Stop it!" she shouted, in exaggerated loudness. "Stop it, Mark! Mom! Mark's shoving me again!"

I heard him give her a good shove and say, "Get away from me, you fat dwarf! And stop answering the door. I told you I would." He came into view. "Hey," he said.

"Hey."

"Sorry about my sister."

"She was okay," I said. "I have one, too."

"Yeah, well she doesn't know when to get lost," he said, opening the screen door.

"Anyone here yet?" I asked as we headed down the carpeted stairs to the playroom.

"Sort of," he said. "Alan Bundy and this girl you don't know from Bay Shore."

Alan, too, was from Bay Shore, but for some reason always found some legal way to come along on our school field trips. He was overweight and had greasy long hair and somehow always reminded me of a fifty-year-old comedian you might see on the *Ed Sullivan Show* a few years ago. One of those old Borscht Belt comedians, but if they were stuffed into a ninth grade long-haired body and had smoked a bunch of marijuana.

Or so it was said. Alan never had any marijuana on him, but the reputation he had was of a proud, regular user who somehow managed to do well in school anyway while charming the teachers with jokes. When you sat next to Alan on one of the field trips, you could be guaranteed he would start with one-liners he'd picked up from watching other comedians' routines, even though he was also at work, he said, on his own original material. "I tell you, it ain't easy being me," he'd begin, sounding more like Rodney Dangerfield than Dangerfield did. "I'm all right now, but you should've seen me last week ... The other day I got in an elevator in my apartment building and the elevator man looks at me and says, 'Basement?'"

This was all funny on a field trip to Albany, but it wasn't the same thing as hanging out with Marie Pappas or my Seven Minutes in Heaven reverie.

The girl next to him, Robin Minsk, knew Mark from youth group at the Reform Temple. (I had stopped going, but Mark said his parents made him still go.) Robin had perfected the art of the bored look by seventh grade, and she always also looked like something around her might have smelled bad a second ago, as her nostrils curled up and away from her slightly downturned lips. It wasn't a very inviting look. On the other hand, she was blonde, which was a bit of a novelty for the girls from the youth group at the Reform Temple.

Mark sat next to Robin, and I sat next to Alan. "Honky Tonk Woman" came across the radio of Mark's crappy portable stereo – the cowbell at the beginning always got me feeling hopeful – and Alan greeted me with, "What a crowd, what a crowd ... I tell you, last week, I told my wife I needed a home improvement loan. She gave me one thousand dollars to move out."

"Hey, Alan. How's Bay Shore treating you?"

"No complaints, no complaints. Of course I shouldn't tell jokes about my wife… I mean, she's attached to a machine that keeps her alive… the *refrigerator*… I tell you, my wife, she can't cook either. She's such a bad cook, a terrible cook. How bad? In my house, we pray *after* we eat…"

"You're not married, Alan. None of us are. We're in ninth grade," I said. "It's a weekend night at Mark's house in ninth grade. Are you practicing for the *Sullivan* show?"

"I'm working on my rhythms," he said in a different voice. "Give me a break here, okay?"

I looked at Robin, scanning the room, desperately looking for anyone else to arrive. Either I hadn't made much of an impression on her, or this was her go-to bored look that could mean anything or everything. She glanced at her wrist quickly, checking the time.

Mark's little sister came trotting down the stairs carrying a big bowl of onion dip. "Mom said to bring this down," she said, anticipating his reaction.

"Put it down and get out of here!" he said.

She did.

Almost immediately the doorbell rang. Mark's sister shouted, "I'll get it!"

Mark sprang to his feet to beat her to the door. "Leave it!" he shouted. "Don't you have any homework?"

"It's the weekend. I already did it," she shouted back.

Mark screamed, "Well, do it again! I told you to get lost!," before we heard the sound of bodies getting slammed up against the wall, much scuffling, and finally seeing her appear on the steps leading to downstairs, running away from Mark at warp speed. "Get up here!" he was yelling. "Don't go downstairs! My friends are down there."

This time his sister ran over to the seat next to Robin

Minsk and sat down defiantly. Robin turned to look at her, her nostrils slightly flaring in an upward direction. "Hi, I'm Elena," the little girl said, as if she were trying to imitate a new classmate of Robin's. Robin turned her head just a half inch and opened her mouth to talk, and that's when she got hit in the head by the flying shoe – a maroon-colored penny-loafer – that had violently and wildly been thrown in his sister's direction.

Robin threw her hands to her face and howled as the shoe bounced away, looking like it was doing a slow loop-de-loop high in the air before landing, with a deep plop, in the bowl of onion dip that was on the side table. Onion dip splattered all over the rest of the table.

Robin stood up, waving her hands in the direction of her face, crying and snuffling back sobs. "Where's a phone? Get me a phone. That might've broken my nose. Who threw that? Who *threw it*?"

Mark stood there with his mouth open, as the late arriving guests, who'd now walked down the stairs to see what all the excitement was, stood next to him.

"My brother did," shouted his sister, rising and striding across the room slowly, elbowing him as she walked up the stairs and away. "My brilliant, brilliant brother. Aren't you impressed? Mark can throw a shoe! He just can't hit the right target, though."

Robin ran upstairs to use a phone. I think she called her mother, because we didn't see her again for the rest of the night. I scanned the new arrivals, looking for Kendra's tall frame, dark hair, and big smile as they appeared at the top of the stairs. Either that or Marie's dark-Italian smoothness. I imagine Marie might be feeling a little out of place here, because she wasn't a big friend of Mark's, whereas Kendra was. I hoped they weren't walking in together.

They weren't. Neither one was there. In walked Brianna Schmidt, a tough girl with a tight, unhappy face, in an Islip High School windbreaker. Next came Mary and Maggie Meisler (identical twins, who'd switch places in classes now and then, to prove that the teachers couldn't tell) and finally, Wendy Pesi, a not very smart girl who'd gotten in trouble last year for a three-way girl fight in the lunchroom. Of all of the arrivals, Wendy at least provided some visual interest, as she was wearing a white peasant blouse that highlighted her bust, along with tight jeans. The twins wore some dumb JCPenney's outfits, with their little scarves pushed in different directions so as not to be completely identical. Before I knew it, Wendy was moving in on me.

"Hi. I'm Wendy."

"Hi, Wendy. I've seen you around."

"Yeah. We have study hall together," she said, filling up an empty cup with Hawaiian Punch. "Want some?" she asked, holding the cup up toward me.

"No, I'm good."

"How's the party so far?" she asked.

"Well," I said, gesturing with my nose in the direction of the shoe in the onion-dip. "That's been the high point so far."

"You mean ... before I got here," she said, laughing and suddenly leaning into me. "Isn't this supposed to be a *pool* party?"

Creedence's "Bad Moon Rising" came on over the stereo.

"Mark didn't even show us where it is," I said.

"Mark!" she shouted. "Where's the pool? Are we going in or not?" Wendy asked. She looked me directly in the eyes. "Did you wear your suit?"

Somehow this suddenly sounded like the sexiest thing I'd ever been asked.

"No. I brought it," I said, motioning to the bag slumped

over in the corner that I'd also brought the trail mix in,

"Why don't you go change?" she asked.

"Okay," I said, going for the bag. I walked past her holding it, and she touched my

arm. "Want company?" she asked.

"You mean ... changing?"

She didn't say anything.

"I'll be right out," I said, moving down the hall hardly believing my ears.

I stayed in the bathroom awhile, checking how my swimsuit looked from different angles, trying it with my shirt on over it, versus just carrying it. I had heard what I heard: Wendy had asked to come in with me while I changed. Did I just miss the opportunity of a lifetime? What would've happened in here? What was supposed to happen next? I needed a pep talk. But I was the only one who could give it. Were you supposed to say things to yourself that were true? Or just hopeful? "You can do this," I said quietly. "She likes you. A lot. You already passed the test. Just be cool. Walk through the party straight to the pool. Go in the pool quickly; she's probably waiting for you there." But I still wanted Marie or Kendra to show up and sidetrack my plans with Wendy.

I came out after changing in the bathroom, my shirt casually unbuttoned but still on, and walked out back toward the pool. It looked like things were going in the direction of getting into the pool fast now. The pool itself – a decent but not large above ground circular thing without a fancy ladder – took up almost one-third of their tiny backyard.

I know that Mark was self-conscious about his father being a milkman or something, driving into the city early every morning and not earning a lot of money while his mother stayed at home smoking cigarettes and watching TV. This was not a deluxe pool in any way.

Brianna – who had changed upstairs, I guess, was in a tight little green two-piece and already in the pool. She still looked like she would punch you in the face in a second or lunge if you said the wrong thing to her. I kept my distance, but came into the water. The pool was lukewarm up to my ankles, then my knees, then rising up my thighs, until I was waist deep. Now what? What are you supposed to do exactly at an aboveground pool party? The answer was partially provided by Alan, who when he came in, dressed in denim jean shorts, his underwear showing up over the waist line, still wearing his T-shirt obviously to cover up his weight, jumped onto my shoulders, pushing my head underwear forcefully. Underwater I could hear him, muffled, shouting, "What a crowd! What a crowd!"

I came up sputtering, "Get off me, Alan! Go do your routine on the Meislers."

"Don't mind if I do," he said, imitating W. C. Fields and tipping the ash off the end of his make-believe cigar, swim-walking away from me. "Don't mind if I do," he said, with some effort lifting his soaking frame out of the pool.

Where did Wendy go? Where was Marie? Where was Kendra?

Where was Mark even?

Suddenly Wendy appeared walking out in a dark blue two-piece. The bottom was pulled up high, accentuating her very long legs. She walked forward with confidence, looking like one of those shampoo ads. It looked like she had, in fact, brushed out her hair, too, or used some sort of spray on it to make it flow long and easily onto her shoulders. She didn't look at all like a ninth grader. Maybe she'd been left back?

The sun was going down now and the last mosquitos of the day were getting their bites in. I was aware of people hopping in and out of the pool, but wasn't keeping track of it, because I was hypnotized by the way Wendy was walking toward me, happily and carrying two cups, which she perfectly balanced while walking up and down the cheap ladder, the water meeting and caressing her thighs as she closed the distance between us and stopped right in front me, almost touching. "Try this," she said, holding out a very full cup.

I did. I lifted it to my lips. It immediately burned and tasted gross enough to make me choke.

"Just chug it," she said.

"What is it?" I asked, slugging the remainder of the cup down my throat, feeling the burn and hoping there was some great payoff to this.

"Southern Comfort," she said.

"What's that?" I asked.

"Magic," she said, her head turning to the side, her lips moving toward me, brushing my face, my skin, finding my lips, and opening. She bore in hard, her lips maybe even saying the word "magic" again as they opened to me, her tongue flicking over and around mine, mine poking back. Before I could really process this, I felt her leg rubbing up against mine.

This was something I'd never felt in my life before, as her leg was 100 percent absolutely guaranteed naked and so was mine. And then, suddenly, there was the rest of her, above her leg, the excited, warm, electricity sending a message right through my bathing suit, caressing me and rubbing me softly, then hard, as her hips ever so slightly did their part. She kissed me again, and everything felt like a single experience, my first time ever like this, my body and hers, moving together, me getting hard and she getting stronger and more insistent with her movements, on and over my leg, her turning me to face her even more, almost fully, her offering up full contact of the front of her body with mine, everything melting together, but not melted, everything getting stiff together, or half-stiff, half-melted, directed by our kisses, all focused on our kisses, now all focused on the front of our bodies as they wanted to complete the turn to be pressed against each other fully. I hugged her and let my hands rest on the lower back part of her suit. *Now what,*? I wondered. *Now what*?

It was somewhere in between almost completely dark and completely dark now. Crickets were chirping in the background. A half-moon was out and Mark's family had Tiki lights that someone lit.

"Let's stay here forever," Wendy whispered, her lips barely pronouncing the words, as they brushed against mine.

I wondered if she felt, and knew, how hard I had gotten while all this was going on. I knew it was evident – there was no missing it, pressed up against her like this – and I wondered if that was okay with her. I guessed that if she wanted to stay there forever, like that it was okay to stay there forever with me pressed up against her all hard, us breathing in each other's mouths and saying Southern Comfort-y things.

Then Mark's voice rang out. "Wendy, your brother's here. He says to meet him out front *now.* Right now. That's what he said."

She shook her head out of the moment with me and touched me on the chest as she abruptly left. "See you in study hall," she said, smiling.

The water in the pool was lapping quietly against the sides in reaction to Wendy having climbed out of it and jostling it with the ladder. I watched it flow back and forth, its movement causing the slightest rise and fall on where the waterline met my mid-chest. I thought of our Southern Comfort kiss. Of the moment when her lips opened and her tongue entered my mouth.

The air had cooled off now, and the whole top part of me did a little shiver as I realized that the pool water wasn't lukewarm anymore. It was chillier than that, and I went back to wondering what you were supposed to do in an above-ground pool. Swim laps?

I could still smell Wendy's hair. It was like a smell I'd known my whole life. But I didn't really know a thing about her. The teasing excitements of just a few moments ago evaporated and with that all signs of my own physical excitement slipped away. I scanned the sliding door of the back of Mark's house, looking for Marie or Kendra. I wondered what would've happened if Kendra walked in and saw Wendy and me in the pool, Wendy getting all melty against me and me joining her, only with hardness.

What if the way you were supposed to get a permanent girlfriend was more like what Wendy and I had explored, instead of the cat-and-mouse confusion that Kendra and I did every single school year since sixth grade? Suddenly, there was a huge splash and something was pulling at my right ankle, hard, throwing me off-balance. My left ankle was shoved to the side, and I lost contact with the pool floor. I fell sharply sideways and was underwater, mid-shout.

Scrambling to stand, I got a mouthful of cold, chlorinated pool water, which I partially swallowed. Coughing, I heard Alan laughing as he stood up next to me, saying, "Women. Can't live with them, can't live without them. Am I right, or am I right?"

"What is your problem?" I spat out, wiping my eyes and moving away from him.

"The other day I said to my wife, 'Honey, I'm feeling good, I'm feeling okay, I'd like to make love...' and she says to me, 'Okay, I'll leave the room to give you some privacy.' I tell you... I don't get *no respect.'"

"Goddammit, Alan! I saw Dangerfield do that bit on TV, you're not even adding to it, you're just repeating it like one of those kids from the Bluebirds at school. They repeat jokes over and over, getting closer and closer to you, til they're laughing in your face, and their breath smells bad, and you laugh to make them go away. But I'm not going to laugh. It's not funny! We're not married, no one is having sex, and the only true part is that people don't respect you. That's true. You don't even go to our school."

"You're saying I'm an immigrant. One of the poor, huddled masses."

"I'm saying you are an annoying kid from Bay Shore. Why are you not at a Bay Shore party instead of this one? I have no idea. Did they ban you?"

The look on his face changed. The corners of his mouth lowered and his lips came together in seriousness. The corners of his eyes were no longer crinkled with laughter, but flattened out in resignation as his eyes widened fully. He suddenly seemed five years older and a lot sadder. But I didn't stop.

"Were you watching us? Instead of making out with someone on your own? Brianna's there all alone…"

"Yeah, that's not gonna happen," he said in a different voice than the one for his comic monologues. "Tried."

"Sorry," I said.

We stood there quietly, the water getting near cold now.

"I go to the Bay Shore parties, too," Alan said. "Whattaya gonna do? All it takes is one girl saying 'yes.' "

" 'Yes' to what?" I asked.

"I don't know. Whatever they say yes to with other guys."

I considered this. "Maybe we outgrew parties," I offered.

"Now there's a sad thought," Alan said. "Isn't this when

it's supposed to start getting good? Teen years?"

"Don't know. Maybe it's when everyone starts acting like they think it's good, but a few years ago was better."

"What made that better?"

I thought about this. "I used to ride my bike a lot and play army with friends in the woods and glue classic monster models together, like the Creature from the Black Lagoon."

"He was cool. Gills and everything. Did they have him green or black?"

I couldn't remember. I just remember he looked awesome.

"Were those the only models you did?"

"Nope," I said. "I had a great Japanese Zero airplane with decals and a few others from World War I and II."

"You get high on the glue?"

"Nope. But it did stick to my fingers a bunch and drips of it are all over the furniture in my bedroom."

"I used to ask for airplane models for my birthday every year," Alan said. "The decals were always tricky, though. I think my fingers were too fat to get them in the right places."

"I know. I only had about a fifty percent success rate with decals."

"How'd you pick out which planes to get?" he asked.

"War movies."

"I watched a bunch of comedies instead," Alan said. "I mean, obviously."

"Yeah, but most of what you do is from TV, right?" I asked.

"Yeah. I work with whatever I've got." He got quiet and looked sad and tired. His hair was all stringy and down on each side of his head. "Sharon Montlani is hot," he offered.

"Yup," I said.

After a bit I asked, "Was the dip and pretzels the only

thing to eat in there?"

"You mean the Onion Dip de la Shoe?"

"Yes. Anything else?"

"His mother brought down chocolate walnut brownies," Alan volunteered.

"Not the kind you get high from?"

"Have you seen his mother? Um, no."

"Alan, do you really smoke weed?" I asked.

"What do you think?" he asked, seeming to enjoy the question.

I looked at him as I imagined a grownup would. "Yes. I think you do."

"Well, then you would be right," he said.

"You have any with you tonight?"

"No."

"Why not?" I asked.

"Because I smoked it on the way over. I wanted to save some to share, but sometimes I just get … greedy, y'know?"

We looked at each other and then I laughed. He did, too. His laughter shook his whole frame. His eyes seemed like they were celebrating the laughter and that he was pleased to be himself in this moment. *Being high, he was laughing on a whole other level*, I thought. I wondered if I could ever in my life find that level of laughter and release.

"What's the weirdest thing about you you've never told anyone?" I asked, not knowing why.

"You're asking me to tell you right after you insult me?" he asked, suddenly not laughing much.

"I guess so. Sorry about the insulting stuff. I don't like being knocked under water. I had a babysitter who tried to drown me once. She held my head underwater for a really long time. I guess she wanted to see what happened."

"Was she stoned?"

"I don't think so. I don't think they had pot back then."

"Oh, they did," Alan said, knowingly. "They did." He looked at me calmly. "You really want to know? Something weird about me?"

"Yeah."

"Then you have to tell me something about you, too."

"Okay. After you."

Alan wrinkled up his nose and looked up in the sky. "You know that TV show, *The Brady Bunch*?"

"With all the bratty kids?"

"Yeah."

"Well ... you know how lots of people think that the mom is hot?"

"I didn't know that, no."

"Well, to me ... I think Alice, the housekeeper is hotter. I have many fantasies about her. In which I rescue her from that shitty situation, and we get down…"

"Whattaya mean?"

"We do it."

I let this sink in. "Isn't she just making people sandwiches and folding clothes all the time?"

"Yeah. They treat her like shit. But ... that's not all there is to her. There's this inner tiger waiting to get out."

"Huh. Never thought of that ... that way. She's kind of plain looking, Alan."

"You don't know much about how sex really works, do you?"

I didn't say anything.

"Plain looking girls can be the hottest ... okay, your turn. What's weird about you?"

"My father has this thing where he hates eating chicken. When he was little they used to raise chickens in the backyard, and they would send him out to select one to kill, and he'd have to wring its neck, then pull the feathers off it, before bringing it in for my grandmother to cook. And he's still not over it. To this day, he hates eating chicken. He avoids it and won't do it."

"Huh."

"But that's not all. Guess what my mother keeps making him for dinner several times a week?"

"Chicken?"

"Yup. She tries to style it up, making things like chicken Polynesian and chicken Hungarian. He comes home, stares at it, and pushes it around with his fork and won't eat it. She sits there and says, 'C'mon, try it, you can hardly taste the chicken.'"

"What's her problem?" Alan asked.

"They hate each other. While they both make believe everything is great. He doesn't talk about the chicken. He occasionally puts out a cigarette in it before the meal is over. And everything is great. We're going to New Hampshire for vacation again this summer."

"Whoa ... not *The Brady Bunch* at your house."

"Nope."

"My parents are divorced. My father is somewhere in Pennsylvania. I think he has a new family."

"That's messed up."

"Yeah."

"You see him at holidays?" I asked. "Your birthday?"

"Nope. I get a card every now and then," Alan said, his face looking long and tired. "Sometimes there's money in it."

"You want to go in?" I asked.

"Yeah," he said, moving his frame slowly up the ladder. "Maybe there are some brownies left."

I followed him and we walked in. The music was loud, only nothing was happening. We both grabbed a brownie and napkins, casually glancing around the room. "Hanky Panky " came on, a perfect dance song, but no one was dancing. Two other boys from the school had arrived while we'd been in the pool, Roy Fine and Eric DeMarco. Both were sitting in chairs looking around, waiting for girls to arrive. Brianna was sitting near them, having changed back into her original party clothes. She was looking around as if she didn't really notice them. The Meislers were saying good-bye and leaving.

"I've played better rooms in Toledo," Alan said, restarting his comedian thing.

"Knock it off, Alan. You've never been to Toledo, and we're not done for the night back here in Islip."

There was one other girl there, Ann LeMarck, a scary smart girl who wore big glasses and never talked to anyone. The only way she was even here was if her parents had forced her to come. She was known to have problems, and kids said she'd been sent to see a therapist in eighth grade after she refused to come to school for three weeks. No one I knew had ever talked to her, and I certainly hadn't. So I sat next to her.

"Hi, how are you?"

She started blushing. "I don't really do these parties," she said, lowering her head and adjusting her hair to cover part of her face more.

Even I knew that this party was seriously in danger of being over before it really started. The only thing saving it was the music, which was all jangly and which suggested that we might be young and cool.

Then Mark's sister came down again. "Mom said you have to turn the music down," she said, coming deliberately close to him to deliver the news with as much punch as she could. "I'm not kidding. She said this is the last warning. She's going to come down and do it. And I told her about the shoe." She turned away and slowly walked up the stairs, like she was daring him to throw something else at her or tackle her.

"It's okay, Mark. Just turn it down," Brianna said, the first words out of her mouth all evening.

And he did. No one was "doing the Hanky Panky" anyway, not here, not anywhere we knew. The song at greatly reduced volume ended, and believe it or not, "The Eve of Destruction" came on.

Mark's sister popped her head downstairs again. "There's a big white car here to pick someone up," she said, directing this to me. "I think it's your mother."

I gathered up my stuff. "Thanks, Mark. Great party."

"No it wasn't," he said, eyes boring into me.

"Yeah it was. Next time there'll be more people."

"It's a Saturday night," he said. "What makes for more people?"

"Gotta go."

I opened the door to my mother's car and slipped in the front seat. "Am I on time?" I asked.

"More or less," she said, starting to drive home.

"Is Dad home?" I asked.

"What do you think?" she answered, staring straight ahead, driving us away.

Primeval Ooze

Music for:
ROCK CONCERTS, DANCES, PARTIES, ETC.

Try Some Today

JERRY   JU 1-1283

In-a-Gadda

# #

It was a Friday and I was home sick. Actually, really sick, not just in need of a break from Mrs Torrence's attempts to show us how to prove that two lines that are parallel to each other never intersect in space, even if extended to infinity (something that had been proven millions of times, I was guessing, by much greater minds than those my tenth-grade buddies and me).

I was in and out of sleep, a fever had its hold over me, and my FM radio was on. I was half-snoring, half-listening to the gargled-in-gravel rumbling voice of Scott Muni introducing something. My mother had been with a tall glass of ginger ale and two Tylenols a few minutes ago, but my forehead was still hot and I went back to dreamland.

I was awakened by the sound of my own Farfisa organ, a nasal, trebly keyboard, piercing through the room, expanding, puncturing through a church-like drone, weaving a melody in between a repeating bass line. But this couldn't be my Farfisa, because I was in bed still, listening, not playing it. Who was playing it?

Then a distorted, electric guitar sound arose like a cobra from the mix, quivering, swinging and swaying, eyes on its prey, lunging, striking, retreating, and repeating, stinging me and startling me out of sleep with its shrill, victorious screams. These folded into oblivion and suddenly all there was was a bass line and drums, then just drums. A mad, simple pounding, a message sent across an ancient forest, tom-toms struck and echoing, new drum smacks layered over the dying notes before it, speaking in code: Wake up, *Wake UP!*

The organ sounds swirled through my room and I realized I was listening to something on WNEW-FM, unlike anything I'd heard before. All rules were out the window now, as the hurricane of sound enveloped me. I could see Kitty Colucci, in her violet miniskirt, in my room, dancing wildly, blonde hair cascading out in all directions, as her body aligned itself with the underlying motions of the universe, which according to Jim Morrison, had to do with sex and… *doing it.* Almost here, almost real, because of this music, conjured up through Farfisa notes, guitar howls, throbbing drum beats and a pulsing bass.

My room turned into a Moroccan marketplace, with strange colors and scents as the organ turned from Arabic to Christian-churchy for a moment, before the return of the electric cobra guitar, and everything fell into place, with vocals layered on top (what on earth *was* he singing?). It swelled, rising in controlled wildness, now bursting out my door then, to my utter shock almost ending with four bars of D-minor arpeggios, *the very thing Mrs. Ketcham had me practicing the week before*. Up, down, over and out, and the song was finally over.

"In-A-Gadda-Da-Vida," Scott Muni croaked, his whiskey-worn voice pronouncing it and making it official for all time. "Iron Butterfly." And my mind was blown open to dimensions I couldn't describe.

Those were arpeggios. The same ones that left my fingers every week.

I called David. "Do you know anything about Iron Butterfly?" I asked. He didn't. I called Paul. "You ever hear of Iron Butterfly?"

"Nope. Maybe you dreamt then. You're home sick, right? You high on something?"

"Yeah. Tylenol."

"What's the name of the song?" he asked.

"Not sure. 'In the Garden of something,'" I guessed.

"I'll look into it," he said and hung up.

He called back within ten minutes. "In-A-Gadda-Da-Vida," he said.

"Yes!" I said. "How'd you find out?"

"Stony Brook's college radio station. I know people who know people. You owe me."

"What kind of name is that?"

" 'In the Garden of Eden,' drunk and stoned-style," he explained.

"Makes sense," I said, hanging up.

On Saturday morning, at 11:00 – just when they opened – I rode my bike to the record store on Main Street in East Islip and bought the album. That's when I first discovered that the song was over seventeen minutes long.

The D-minor arpeggios of "In-A-Gadda-Da-Vida" kept echoing through my mind – while sitting in English class, playing dodgeball in gym, or riding my bike home from school.

I had a new band now to bring my Farfisa to. Connections at BayWay Beach Club brought me into the world of a bass-player/drummer pair of brothers, and they knew two kids who went to Catholic school in Nassau County who played guitars and had real connections. Connections who could get us jobs at CYO dances at church halls. We just had to learn some songs first. Of course though, we were obsessed with getting a name first. Just like the old band.

We thought of everything weird we could, but our world of weird was limited to high school and what we saw and heard of other bands. The formula seemed to be choosing two words that formed an opposite kind of trippy-mind synthesis, like Iron Butterfly.

Mike suggested "Dirt Babies" (I don't know why) and Alex threw "Harmonic Distortions" into the mix. Terry stared blankly off into the distance at Saturday morning rehearsal in my basement before offering "Snot Attack," then saying he was kidding. We all looked to Ron, who said, "I dunno, let's just play, okay? Why do we need to come up with it right now?"

"Because we have a gig two weeks from now at St. Lawrence's CYO in Sayville," Randy said.

"We do?" I asked. "How'd we get that?"

"My mother. She knows someone who knows someone," Alex said. "They need a name."

"Okay, how about this?" I asked, thinking about Mr. Bezelman's science class and the almost monster-movie weirdness of his lectures. "Primeval Ooze."

Terry nodded, maybe because it seemed to have something to do with snot in his mind. Alex twisted his head some and scrunched up his features, unsure. But Ron and Mike nodded. Ron said, "That's okay."

"What does it mean?" Alex asked.

"It's where we all came from," I said. "Before Nassau and Suffolk counties. It's where all life came from."

"Okay, weird. That's good for now," Mike said. "Now can we learn some songs?"

We each chose four songs to learn – all covers of other people's stuff – and we'd each take responsibility for teaching each other the chords. That way we'd have about twenty songs by the following week.

The next week came and Ron and Mike started crunching out "Sunshine of Your Love," jamming over it and playing it longer and longer until they got tired of it. I asked about the four songs apiece thing we were supposed to learn and teach by today, and everyone looked down. The good idea had died on the vine. In addition to "Sunshine of Your Love" and "Spoonful" – a two-chord song I never understood and grew to truly hate, even when Cream was playing it – we had three other solid oldies and two songs that fell apart after the first eight bars or so.

I seemed to be the only one who was really concerned about this, imagining us at the CYO dance next week getting introduced and running out of things to play in thirty minutes while getting paid $75 to play for three hours. So I spoke up. "I know two songs can give us more than a half hour."

Mike snorted.

"If we jam," I said.

"On what?" Ron asked.

" 'In-A-Gadda-Da-Vida' and 'Light My Fire.' "

They were quiet.

"You know them?" Alex asked.

"Yuh."

"Are they hard to learn?" Mike asked skeptically.

"A little. To get 'em to sound good, yeah. But we can get the basic stuff in by next week if you stop playing 'Spoonful' and want to learn." I sounded like a grown-up.

So we worked on them and after an afternoon of relatively focused attention and practice, they both sounded pretty bad. "Light My Fire" sounded like noise – even though my keyboard introduction was perfect – after the guitars came crunching in, smashing the chords with bulldozer-like subtlety, and the singer constantly missed the cues to come in again after the long soloing.

"In-A-Gadda-Da-Vida" sounded like a long night of fifteen-year-olds with instruments, drinking, then stumbling towards their amps in the middle of that night. And maybe they'd picked up their instruments for the third or fourth time ever. Only not as good as that. But Alex got the drum solo idea pretty fast. My attempts to duplicate a Moroccan marketplace with my keyboard ended up sounding more like a confused kid from Long Island's imitation of a kitten crawling both ways across random amplified keyboard keys. It was halfway between something and nothing, which put it in the gentle train wreck category. At least we ended the song at the same time.

We laughed, and Ron said, "Get a piece of paper and write the set list."

One thing that the CYO dance meant – and we all knew it – was lots of girls dancing. The combination of us playing loud music, getting money – $15 a person at least, likely more, plus dancing girls ... It just didn't get much better than that.

During our pizza break at Mike's Pizza, where the olive oil dribbled down your hand as you held the slice and moved it to your mouth was the mark of quality to us, Alex pressed Ron and Mike hard.

"So Catholic girls? What is it with them again?"

"They've got this pent-up energy," Mike offered. "So when they get a chance to go crazy, they do."

We pondered this.

"Like ... How crazy?" Terry asked.

"*Crazy*. You'll see."

No one in the room was saying it but we all thought about Donna, Ron's girlfriend. She was an emotional rollercoaster everytime we saw her. She'd come to practice with Ron sometimes, help him set up his equipment, bark at him for not being organized, then interrogate him about his plans for after practice, run off in a huff if he didn't answer her fast enough, cry for reasons none of us could determine, and in between hang out leaning against the wall watching us play, nodding her head and half-dancing.

The presence of an actual girl half-dancing to our stuff motivated us toward even higher levels of beginner-music status, as we could see the straight path in between Donna moving to our music to thousands of girls doing the same. It suddenly seemed possible that if we could fill an entire set list, we could join with the crazy Catholic girls of Sayville next week, play "Light My Fire," and give them permission – since the story was that they'd already be likely to have hiked their skirts up higher than they were when they'd left home – to lose their minds in a large group. "In-A-Gadda-Da-Vida" would push them over the edge, and they'd take us with them. There was a direct link between this stuff and sex.

Our set list ended up being short, but it took us longer to set up our equipment on two different sets of risers than we'd thought and a last minute search for extension cords took twenty minutes of the dance's time, which the kids at the dance didn't seem to mind, because the guitarists were constantly tuning up, then playing snippets of "Sunshine of Your Love" and oh no – "Spoonful."

Donna seemed to be stage managing our setup, getting into a yelling match with Terry at one point, telling him that he was set up too close to Ron and that it looked stupid. He imitated her voice: "You're *too frickin' close,*, Terry!"

She stormed off after saying fast, "Why do you always have to be such a stupid bastard?" Her miniskirt swung in the breeze around her as she exited.

After about another fifteen times of the guitarists tuning up, we finally launched our first song: "Evil Ways," by Santana. And *boom* – just like that, the girls were there, in front of us, dancing, as we'd hoped. Alex sunk into the groove of the song in a steady way and Rob actually sounded good, Mike a little clunky, and the organ sound was as close as I could get to a Hammond, waiting for my solo. It was all happening and happened and was smooth as silk and when the song was over, there was actual applause and hoots and hollers.

I don't have any memory of guys being there, but they had to have been there, as well. But there were *lots of girls*.

We were a part of all this. We were okay. We were cool.

During the second break we took, we learned that three girls had been thrown out by school assistant principals for being drunk. This was getting cooler by the moment.

We saved "In-A-Gadda-Da-Vida" for the last set. That turned out to be the right move because by that point in the night, with their parents lining up to pick them up outside in a few minutes and deliver them back to safe, suburban homes – it was now or never for going crazy, and they went crazy.

Ron had bought a fuzz-box that week and had mastered sounding weird with it. The distorted fuzz-tones Ron was putting out layered over Terry's rock-solid bass line, and my trebly nasal fake Middle Eastern churchy lines and Mike's sloppy singing had everyone united in whatever this was, ready to follow us over a cliff if we led them, but they were leading us as much as we were leading them, and we were caught in a moment where there were no leaders or followers anymore, just a bunch of dancing teenage bodies, not ready to stop, refusing to have the song be over, which was good, because Alex's jungle drum solo was only about halfway through the whole thing and when we came in after it, all together, it felt like we were raising the roof of St. Lawrence's martyrs and replacing it with our screaming energy, which would continue for all time, past when we turned twenty-one, past when we would turn thirty-five or fifty, past when we would turn sixty.

We would never grow old because of this moment and being fully alive in this moment guaranteed it. We were

Primeval F'ing Ooze, and it felt like all of later life would come from this loud, churning, earthy mess.

We got asked back. They wanted us for three more dates, spread out over the next year. This was the big time.

From that point on, we were no longer regular high schoolers. We were high schoolers in a band. The civilian part of our lives was about homework, tests, and taking the garbage out on Wednesday nights. The rock-star parts of our lives was about what gigs we had scheduled for the next three months. And lo and behold, our Fridays and Saturdays started filling up. We now had girls coming to hang out and watch us during our rehearsals, just because... y'know. They wore tight jeans and chewed gum a lot and smelled like shampoo or girls' body sprays.

It was hard to believe it, because we had arrived.

Zeus, The Horse

#

"Samantha has a sister," my father told me. "I don't know how things are between you and Kendra, but Samantha has been talking about you to her sister."

"What did she tell her?" I asked.

"I don't know. If you want to know, ask Samantha."

Samantha was the pharmacy assistant my father had hired to help him count pills, print out labels, package prescriptions, process credit cards, and print out receipts for people. Since she was only seventeen and the only license she had was a driver's license, that meant that my father had to be the one standing next to her and officially counting out the pills before she could put them in the container. They worked shoulder to shoulder when prescriptions came in, and that was most of the time.

He'd told me several times that she was interested in becoming a pharmacist herself someday, and he was trying to encourage that. He didn't explain much, but made it clear that this would really raise her status in life and help her get out on her own.

I was over on aisle four when he'd told me about Samantha's sister, restocking the women's hair coloring products, having brought a ton of things up from the basement in three trips. I worked after school on Tuesdays and Thursdays. Sometimes on Sundays I went with him to work.

"What time is it?" he asked, glancing toward his wrist.

"4:15 p.m.," I quickly offered. "Could I take some licorice?"

This was always a source of some confusion. I had grown up thinking that my father owned the whole place, but then learned that he had a partner, Victor (and maybe even a third one, Gus), and that Victor "held notes" in the place. When I was a bit younger and my father asked if I wanted him to bring anything home for me, I always asked for black licorice, and two or three rolls of 35 mm. camera film. I'd eat the licorice, take creative pictures in black-and-white (later color slides), and give him the film back to be sent out for developing. About five days later, he'd bring home my pictures. I was getting better as a photographer.

Sometimes my mom, sister, and I would give him a whole list of things to bring home for the house, and he would. These would often include antibiotics (unprescribed by any doctor), which he'd bring home for us. These antibiotics were his own idea, meant to help us "catch it early," if we weren't feeling great in any way.

But when I worked in the store with him, especially when Victor was there working with him, and my father asked if I wanted anything (even a snack from the candy rack an hour or two before dinner), I'd notice Victor looking up and keeping track of me.

My father's voice sounded different than when it was just him and me there, or him, me, and Samantha, and sometimes he would change it to "Do you *need* anything?" I would still gather up the 35 mm. film and the licorice, but finally one day I asked him, "Can I pay for these?"

He looked shocked and embarrassed, shaking his head *no* as my question still hung in the air. "No, don't be silly, just take them," he said. Which was a good thing, because I wasn't sure I had enough money in my pocket to have done so, as

ALSO BY THE AUTHOR

"...will bring to mind Phillip K. Dick's work, with all the deceptions, fake realities, and mind-scrambles that entails...Complicated and intelligent post-cyberpunk science fiction."
– KIRKUS REVIEWS

"A masterfully written novel; smart, funny, poignant, and painful..."
– DIANA E. SHEETS

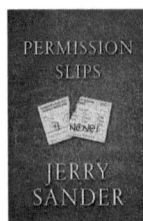

"*Permissions Slips* is not sanitized for one's emotional protection...A dark, sometimes violent story of struggling to maintain a stable life, identity, and maybe even find love amidst the worst youth has to offer."
– MIDWEST BOOK REVIEW

Jerry's books are available in Kindle and print formats via his Amazon author page: https://www.amazon.com/~/e/B004K61EZ0

www.ingramcontent.com/pod-product-compliance
Lightning Source LLC
Chambersburg PA
CBHW070350070426
42446CB00050BA/2785